Polly Toynbee is a political and social commentator for the *Guardian*. Previously she was the BBC's Social Affairs Editor and a columnist for the *Independent* and the *Observer*. She is the author of *Hard Work: Life in Low-Pay Britain*, *Hospital* and *Lost Children*. With David Walker she has written two audits of Labour's first and second terms: *Did Things Get Better?* and *Better or Worse, Did Labour Deliver?*

David Walker edits *Public*, the monthly magazine published by the *Guardian* for senior public sector executives and was formerly chief leader writer of the *Independent*. He is a member of the Economic and Social Research Council, a non-executive director of the National Centre for Social Research and a trustee of the Nuffield Trust for health policy studies. He is author of *The Times Guide to the New British State* and co-author of *Sources Close to the Prime Minister*.

Unjust Rewards

Exposing Greed and Inequality in Britain Today

POLLY TOYNBEE AND
DAVID WALKER

GRANTA

Granta Publications, 12 Addison Avenue, London W11 4QR

First published in Great Britain by Granta Books, 2008

A CIP catalogue record for this book
is available from the British Library.

1 3 5 7 9 10 8 6 4 2

ISBN 978 1 84708 093 6

Printed and bound in Great Britain
by CPI William Clowes Beccles NR34 7TL

Contents

PART FOUR: Just Rewards: Raising the money

Introduction

'How to Spend It', the *Financial Times*'s Saturday supplement, is big money Britain on glossy display. Financial markets have been on a rollercoaster ride since summer 2007 but the cash tills ring on. Flick the pages and admire a Chanel garment with an £8,075 price tag, Casino Royale satin stilettos for £720 or an Dior python-skin handbag for £3,035. A Tourbillon wristwatch costs £200,000. 'Cellar your bonus,' suggests a wine merchant, who offers a personal wine-trainer at £2,500 a day. A spa retreat in Motukawaiti, New Zealand, costs £7,800 a night, or you can heli-ski down live volcanoes in Kamchatka at £2,650 a run. A burgeoning class of merchants now battles for the business of the billionaires, searching out obscure objects to satisfy their every desire. About a hundred of the new generation of pleasure boats called super-yachts were ordered in 1998; nearly 500 in 2008. A concierge company called Quintessentially will do anything, anywhere, for a price – deliver bongo drums to a yacht at sea or, for £25,000 an hour, a premiership footballer for a nine-year-old's birthday.

Here is conspicuous consumption by the City bonus-barons, corporate lawyers, tycoons, hedge-funders and the non-domiciled who enjoy the UK enough to live here, but not enough to join us in paying UK tax. Maybe they do inhabit another country: the UK has become a fissured, unequal place. Of course there has been some progress, and households on below-average incomes saw gains during the decade to 2006, but under Labour the incomes of the top 1% have grown more quickly than those of any other percentile. Rich people are rolling in it: the Institute for Fiscal Studies finds that the top 1% takes 13% of all income and the top 10% take over 27% – and that's only what they declare.[1] Big money could justify itself by claiming these are really special and able people on whose brains and talent the prosperity of the nation depends. But boardroom rewards are what economists call rent, a result of luck and circumstance rather than merit. Top people have become greedy. John Plender is only one of the perspicacious and pro-capitalist commentators worrying in recent times that too many executives 'have come to expect entrepreneurial rewards for managerial performance'.[2] What part did objectively measured worth play in how they got the pelf, what effect will gross affluence have on their pampered children? Trust corrodes and social bonds snap when such pumped-up rewards are paid to the few, undermining the confidence and mutual regard on which markets and the economy depend.

The financial crisis that began with sub-prime lending in the US in April 2007 was retribution. Bonus-fixated bankers retreated so far from the real world that they could not see and perhaps did not even care that poor households could not afford their mortgages: their ignorance precipitated the credit crunch. This absence of social imagination is all too characteristic of the City of London: the UK too illustrates what can happen when the income gap grows between financiers and the people whose everyday pensions, savings and mortgages they manage. Financial *Sturm und Drang* may have begun to slow board-room excess, but have any lessons been learnt?

The ranks of the British rich have been swelling. An estimated 19,000 people declared an annual income in excess of £500,000 in 2003–4. Their numbers grew by 30,000 over the subsequent twenty-four months. The incomes of the top 1% grew half as fast again as average income. This leap in fortune for the few happened during the Tony Blair–Gordon Brown years. Labour was far from inactive: it pushed money towards poorer households and spent more on public services, pushing public spending up to 42% of GDP by April 2008. But the Blairites liked rich people and Brown bought into the specious argument that the country's economic well-being demanded that remuneration committees let rip. Plutocrats came into their own in the midst of the progressives' ostensible triumph.

Think of the UK as a camel train crossing the desert, with the low paid bringing up the rear. The whole thing is moving forward: the economy has been growing and the whole train is better off; even the stragglers have DVD players imported from China in their saddlebags. So those at the back inch forwards too, but far slower than the sheikhs at the front, whose pace has accelerated so fast their dust is barely seen above the far-distant dunes. When can they no longer be said to be travelling in the same caravan at all?

Without anyone quite willing it, the UK has become more divided. Refusing to see any connection between accelerating inequality and the atrophy of common identity, Brown harps on about the importance of citizenship. But increasingly we don't belong to the same community. Modern culture celebrates the demotic, inclusive, non-deferential society, but in social and economic reality a canyon divides moneyed and sub-median-income Britain, and the bridges across crumble and collapse. The net worth of the wealthy swells, while the third of the population with no assets worth counting see their chance of ever owning anything – like a house or flat – diminish further. Money buys an inter-generational advantage too. Birth is now destiny, and the predictive power of family background stronger than at any time since the 1939–45 war. Parental income pretty accurately predicts whether a child will win or lose in life: the more unequally income is shared, the tighter the link becomes. Public rhetoric talks up opportunity just when life chances bifurcate. Out loud the rich mutter a few words acknowledging the poor, the housing estates and the under-achievement, but they also complain about taxes; and in private they say 'So what', our gated houses will protect us and besides, the criminality of the poor mainly afflicts themselves.

Avner Offer, in *The Challenge of Affluence* (2006), noted how, as the income gap expands, higher groups share less and less with the rest of the population. 'In a political process that is responsive to money, the lack of perceived common interests translates into less redistribution and less protection for workers who are losing ground . . . reducing individual opportunity and upward mobility'. The rich are in many ways the problem. Patterns of disadvantage can be broken, but only over time and through social interventions. By the government, or paid for by the government. Their cost will be met by tax; if the system is progressive it bites harder on the very well off. That way the camel train can be drawn back together: bunched closer it will travel faster and in better spirits, safer and happier.

Growing disparity is not in dispute. In a special report on Britain (1/2/07), *The Economist*, hardly a mouthpiece for progressives, noted how income was 'distributed more unequally than in almost any big rich country except America'. Bar Switzerland, the UK is far less equitable than other European countries. The top 10% of income earners get 27.3% of the cake; the bottom 10% get 2.6%. Twenty years ago the average chief executive of one of the top hundred companies on the FTSE index earned 17 times the average employee's pay. By 2008, the typical FTSE boss earned 75.5 times the average, according to the Institute of Directors. The UK is sliding backwards. Already by 1999 the top 10% of taxpayers got a higher share than they did in 1937, before the creation of the welfare state.[3] Trends in holdings of wealth are similar. To visualize what has happened, line up 200 people representing the UK population as a whole; the one person at the top end nets nearly 10% of the total wealth. As for income, out of each extra £100 that national income has grown since 1979, £40 has gone to the top twenty people in the line. Since Labour came to power in 1997 the proportion of personal wealth held by that top 10% swelled from 47% to 54%. Labour did try to tug in the opposite direction, mainly through its tax credits. As described in *The Economist*, 'Over the past decade the move to even greater inequality has been slowed by policies such as the minimum wage and benefits to the poor. Even so the pay of the top earners has rocketed whereas the disposable income of average households has risen only modestly.' To add insult to injury, Gordon Brown's last budget as chancellor axed the 10p tax rate, with the effect of leaving many of the lowest paid without children to bear a heavier burden. The fabric of society is not just fraying; the entire garment is being pulled apart.

Vast sums are being accumulated by families. In May 2007, Rupert Murdoch gave each of his six children £50 million worth of shares. They were perhaps a mere gift, a taster, a simple down-payment on the money they will probably get on his death. The tycoon is an extreme example, but scaled down, such transfers will become more frequent, boosting the dynastic potential of wealth. The wealthy's greatest coup has been to present themselves as somehow typical, or representative of wider society. So Labour, unsure of its own mind, cut inheritance tax although only the richest 6% of estates were ever liable: it was never a Middle England tax. By 2010, instead of a tax exemption on the first £350,000, couples will be able to leave £700,000 in their estates completely untaxed. In 2007 the Conservatives upped the ante, promising £1 million on an individual estate, or £2 million tax-free inheritance for any couple who put their money into tax-planning trusts. Meanwhile, both parties have turned a blind eye to the super-rich who invest money for children in offshore tax-haven trusts.

This regressive tax change will do much to accelerate inequality and reverse the progress that inheritance tax has made over the last century, when it successfully chipped away at feudal fortunes passed from generation to generation. Today we know little of who owns what, as wealth is a submerged Atlantis of property, assets and undeclared income. The Land Registry, ostensibly a bible for ownership records, covers only 50% of the land area of England and Wales.[4] Professor Ian Walker of Warwick University reminded us how little research has been done on the rich. 'The data we have is brain damaged,' and though we can see fairly clearly what people earn up to £250,000 a year, beyond that we are dealing with averages. 'Beware', he said grimly, 'of systematic non-response bias' in surveys of the better off: they don't tell, so the figures we use in this book are certainly gross under-estimates of the property and income divide.

Social mobility is slowing down. Rich parents tend to have children who are rich, particularly in the UK and the US. Policies which try to compensate those children who don't have an advantaged home – funding their early-years and nursery education, extra help at school and access to university – need to be extraordinary to counteract this growing social disadvantage. Welcome measures, such as the expansion of higher education, turn out to benefit those from better-off backgrounds most. Sociologists note that, despite all the talk about its decline, family is stronger than ever in determining where children end up in life. Genes play their part, but when Gary Solon of the University of Chicago studied adopted children he found strong evidence that life chances are deeply affected by the wealth of the home the child is raised in.[5] Parents' education predicts the literacy level of their children much better in the UK than in Japan or Sweden.[6] Poor parents beget poor children, not because they lack ability or aspiration but because they haven't got the money that ensures a decent start in life. Shockingly, the UK rates last among twenty-one rich countries as a good place for children to grow up.[7] A UNICEF study showed how the lives of children mirror those of adults in a society where the rewards for success are hugely disproportionate to effort or merit, while the penalties for ending up on the minimum wage are inexplicably unjust.

Ideas of what are ordinary or fair rewards spin like a compass that has lost its magnetic north. 'Performance pay' is an oxymoron because the executives and directors awarded it get far more than their objectively measured contribution to an organization would justify. Discontent grows amid social unease, helping explain the marked growth in general 'distrust' in recent years. People who get less routinely resent their workplace. The annual British Social Attitudes Survey has shown a consistently high number of people think the gap between top and bottom too wide – 76% in the 2007–8 findings. The *Guardian*'s ICM poll (19/2/08) showed its highest ever score for concern about the widening gap, at 75%. It's not just people of liberal disposition: wherever they stand on the political spectrum, most believe there is a breaking point. Modernity holds that individuals should have the chance to give life their best shot, and a crack at success. No economy can compete and prosper if talent is stifled or opportunity denied to anyone with something to contribute – and that means all but a tiny hardcore of dysfunctional people. The UK in the twenty-first century should be a place where people can move on and up.

But it isn't, despite the policy initiatives of recent years. Results may not show for a generation, but public investment has so far produced only modest improvement. Social mobility is barred. Where people are born, there they are destined to remain, more fixed than even thirty years ago. The fifteen-year boom in house prices from the mid-1990s, so loved by home-owners, has cemented people even more rigidly to their class. Data are patchy but Jo Blanden of the University of Surrey says it stretches credulity not to associate soaring house prices with reduced social mobility, because capital passes on to children of the 70% who are home-owners, while nothing is received by children of the rest.

History, many like to believe, is a Whiggish tale of growing wealth, social progress and fairer distribution, an onward march from Factory Acts to the founding of the welfare state. We all wear the same clothes, listen to the same music, meet on equal terms in Facebook and MySpace. Yet our background predicts who will run the investment banks and who will clean their floors; it's not happenstance, it is largely pre-programmed. Sure, Sir Alan Sugar pulled himself up from a poor background. Individuals can make it, just as anyone can win the lottery. It could be you, but the odds are heavily stacked against it. General mobility is a myth.

Class as it used to be experienced has changed. Between the 1950s and 1970s the labour market was remoulded as old industrial and manual jobs disappeared and office work expanded, often requiring more formal education. A two-thirds working-class society became two-thirds white collar. Mass unemployment in the 1980s hit hard those on the wrong side of the transition. At exactly the same time the deregulation of finance blew the lid off boardroom earnings. The top rate of income tax was cut by the Thatcher government in the first post-1979 election budget from 83% to 60%. Then it was cut again in 1986 to 40%, where it remains, one of the lowest maximum rates of income tax in Europe. In 1979 the UK was one of the more equal developed nations, though one in seven children still grew up poor. But in the 1980s more and more households fell into poverty and by the early 1990s one in three children lived below the poverty line, relegating the UK to near the bottom of developed countries.

Those ratios tell only half the story. The other half is cultural and attitudinal. With the working class a minority, those on low incomes are despised, whether they work or don't work. We need people to clean hospitals, care for the elderly, check out at supermarket tills, clerk the offices, labour on building sites, assist the teachers and sweep the streets. We can't do without them, yet their paltry pay devalues the work they do, and the poor have been excluded. They live in an archipelago of estates that are feared for their disorderliness; their children are consigned to schools the rest take pains to avoid. The contours of this other world are varied but its inhabitants, a third of the nation, hold too little power now to command respect and few are now represented by power-broking trade unions. They have become the butt of snobbery by the new middle class, mocked as chavs, Spudulikas, hoodies and low-lifes, portrayed as drunken scroungers on the TV series *Shameless*, their tastes laughed at in class-shock reality shows such as *Wife Swap*. Though most people in minimum-wage jobs strive hard, these unrepresentative, grotesque images encourage a smug sense that all the poor are 'people not like us'.

Crime as recorded by the police and assessed in surveys has

been falling since the 1990s, yet fear has grown. The well off don't sleep easy in their beds, unless they are padlocked and gated in. Popular consciousness is populated with the spectres of hoodies, teenagers, 'the others' prowling outside the gates. Inequality sharpens this social anxiety and the panicky sense that things are falling apart. The greater the gap between the home-owner and the estate-dweller, the deeper the alarm, never mind the figures or the (lowered) probability of becoming a victim of crime.

A child from a family getting by on around £200 a week has known from the first day at school what it feels like to be worth less. This child has no birthday parties, no holidays, no plane or even train rides, no Xbox games that other children talk about and no computer for online chatting. Facebook is a closed book. Shop windows, television images and play-ground conversation all painfully remind this child that she is excluded from the mainstream. Is it surprising that a few of these children will devise for themselves the private gang culture that causes a national outcry? It makes sense that young people with nothing, no power and few prospects, will create their own surrogate systems of status and reward, fighting for the respect they get nowhere else. If esteem is something humans cannot live without, then it can seem worth dying for. Adam Smith called this basic human need 'the pursuit of regard'.

Human behaviour has a mirror in our relatives, the monkeys. At London Zoo a compound houses the macaques – tufted monkeys with long lugubrious faces. The troop has a male and four females, one with a baby clinging to her belly as they swing from bar to ledge. Jo, the macaques' keeper, watches over them. If a monkey sinks low in the hierarchy it may fall into depression, risking its health and well-being. In an experiment, macaques were shifted around different troops, their social position altering as previous high rankers lost status in a new group. In *The Impact of Inequality: How to make sick societies healthier* (2005), Richard Wilkinson described a social gradient among the monkeys and the finding that status anxiety is toxic. After just twenty-one months the animals which moved down the social scale, although given identical food, suffered a five-fold increase in heart disease due to raised cortisol levels produced by extra stress. Low-status monkeys and low-status humans suffer the same diseases.

Michael Marmot, in *Status Syndrome* (2004), looked at the health of civil servants over two decades and found the clerks and messengers far more likely to suffer ill health than the principals, let alone the permanent secretaries. Screening out other causes, he found that lack of respect causes disease. Raised levels of stress hormones are implicated in the premature deaths of poor people in rich societies and status is correlated with heart disease. Stress is not related to how much people have to live on; poor people in poor countries fare better in measured health and well-being relative to their fellow citizens than better-off people at the bottom of the ladder in rich countries. It is relative income and comparative social standing that matter, not absolute standard of living. Those with most control over their life and work thrive, while the powerless and despised suffer. One implication of these findings is that the cost of healthcare could be lower in a more equal society. Lessening inequality could cut demand; seeking social change is going to be better value than spending on the NHS. Perhaps historians will judge Labour's increase in health spending from 6% to 8% of GDP as a mistake. This was consumption, not investment in the future. Doctors, hospitals and drugs may be in demand but they don't address the underlying causes of ill health and lack of well-being – and doctors are usually the first to say so. The answer to better health is out there, in society itself.

Avner Offer argues that there is 'little doubt about the costs of inequality and insecurity: being low down the scale of absolute income is associated with misery: with shorter lives, bad health, discrimination, poor education, incarceration, and other detriments. GDP per head is a fiction, no one earns GDP per head.'[8] If increments in GDP per head in the years after the 1980s contributed virtually nothing to subjective well-being while increases in inequality were positively harmful, then the rise in GDP left society worse off.

Growing inequality in income and wealth undermines democracy. Grandiose promises of equal human rights and civic equality dissipate when it is money that secures political power. Wealth buys access to ministers, dinners at the House of Commons and privileged exemptions from law and regulation. Above all, the rich can shield themselves against taxation. The American heiress Leona Helmsley exaggerated in saying 'only the little people pay taxes' – the UK system remains broadly 'progressive' in that higher incomes pay higher rates of tax. But the rich chip away. Even if they are not actively disloyal – taking money out of the country and sequestering it in tax havens abroad – they threaten to jump ship at any suggestion that rates might change.

Democracy is egalitarian – one person, one vote. But wealth makes some votes more influential than others. A paradigm case of wealth's twenty-first-century access to politics is Silvio Berlusconi, who used his money and media power to found a party and become prime minister, altering tax laws to suit his purse and other laws to give him immunity from prosecution over business dealings. Rupert Murdoch, who pays virtually no tax in Britain, has no need to enter politics himself: he can use his editors to bring government ministers to heel in Australia, the US and the UK. Money's political sway is set to grow if the children and grandchildren of billionaires do not stick to owning football clubs.

Yet the rich have been unable to stop themselves and their privileges entering the mainstream of political conversation. Under David Cameron the Tories have accepted there is a problem. The image of society as a camel train – coined in *Hard Work: Life in Low-pay Britain* (2003) by Polly Toynbee – was lifted by the leadership, who said that modern Tories now realized it was important that the poor at the back of the train never fell too far behind. But what of the rich galloping ahead? Oh no, Cameron hastened to say, that's no problem.

The governments led by Blair and Brown cannot fairly be accused of ignoring inequality: Blair's commitment to the abolition of child poverty was a striking promise, showing as bold a vision as the inventor of the welfare state, David Lloyd

14

George. But Labour's approach was also illustrated by the remark of Blair's sidekick Peter Mandelson, who was 'relaxed about people getting filthy rich'. This sentiment has been repeated at intervals by such keepers of the Blairite flame as John Hutton, the business secretary, who in March 2008 said 'rather than questioning whether huge salaries are morally justified, we should celebrate the fact that people can be enormously successful in this country'. Here is Labour's version of Mrs Thatcher's dictum about there being no such thing as society, as if no connection existed between the poor, the sub-medians and their life chances, and the tax not paid by the rich.

New Labour's anachronism is proved when Sir Samuel Brittan, an implacable economic liberal, says 'we can no longer say with as much confidence as before that redistribution will achieve very little' (*Financial Times*, 10/2/06), although no one now proposes squeezing the rich until the pips squeak, in Denis Healey's immortal phrase. With so many more of them, gentle pressure would go a long way. Tax consultants Grant Thornton estimated that the UK's fifty-four billionaires paid income tax of only £14.7million in 2006 on fortunes totalling £126 billion. At least thirty-two paid no income tax at all and very few paid any capital gains tax, so Leona Helmsley would be gratified. To give some idea of the potential that could be harvested from the wealthy, take the 1,000 people who appeared in the *Sunday Times* Rich List for 2007, from A for Abramovich (£10.8 billion) to Z for Zwanziger (£100 million). If in 2007 Her Majesty's Revenue & Customs had secured the 10% of their capital gains and 40% of their higher-bracket income as Parliament ordained, the Treasury would have been better off by £12 billion, simply by collecting what is avoided. Add in tax avoided by companies through various legal loopholes, and tax expert Richard Murphy estimates £25 billion could be recouped.

Redistributed, this largesse would pay for social progress. According to the Institute for Fiscal Studies, £3.4 billion a year would lift enough families out of poverty to hit Labour's pledge of halving child poverty by 2010. The rest could fund intensive early help for children from poor families, giving them a better start in life. Social policies that work rely on high spending and a particular effort to rescue those in danger of failure, with professional family therapists, drug and alcohol addiction treatments and children's centres.

Change starts with consciousness, and this book has been written as an optical aid, to sharpen ways of seeing society's misshapenness. In the following pages the rich and the poor are on display. What happened in the boardrooms that permitted the explosion in rewards? What does it feel like to be a master of the universe, and is that how City high-flyers see themselves? And what is it like to live under the poverty line? Behind the statistics we discover the attitudes and experiences that make up our society today. We explore what can be done to make Britain fairer, and which polices work to bring people closer together. We will unpack two myths that help keep things the way they are. One says this is already a land of opportunity, if only people at the bottom would aspire and try harder. The other says inequality is functional, a necessary precondition of the economic success from which everyone benefits – except they don't. This UK camel train is somewhere near breaking point: only the dust kicked into their eyes stops those in the back half seeing how the front riders have already abandoned the rest of the community on its journey.

PART ONE

The Camel Train: The leaders gallop away

CHAPTER 1

Who do the super-rich think they are?

From the marbled twentieth floor of a glass tower in Canary Wharf the view of the river is breathtaking. It snakes down to the Thames barrier, glinting in the sunset. Close to the new city lie the serried ranks of East End estate blocks. The view is typical of London: glossy new wealth nestling close to old and persisting penury. Precious little money has trickled down from this gilded new town in the sky to its neighbours below.

High earners tend to be cannily elusive, preserving their privacy at home and at work, journeying between them in expensive cars. Only through cajolery and persuasion did we manage to collect together a group of masters of the universe willing to open themselves to our gaze, expound their attitudes on pay and expose their knowledge of the society we live in. We wanted to ask how they accounted for their extraordinary incomes and good fortune. What, to them, was fair – and what might persuade them to share more of their largesse with others? They agreed to meet, on condition that we did not name them or their firms.

These City high-flyers were not briefed in advance, so they didn't know what they would be asked. We set about our task with some trepidation; these days it feels almost impertinent to challenge those who rule the roost ideologically as well as economically, and here were people not used to confronting inconvenient social facts.

Were they going to be typical of the population at large? The general public deny that anyone these days is poor; or if they are, then believe it is their own feckless fault.[1] 'Poverty' conjures images of African babies, and the notion of relative poverty in the modern UK appears hard to grasp. Eurobarometer's surveys consistently show people in the UK to be most punitive towards the poor, despite or because of higher proportions living below the poverty line than in most other EU countries. But the general public will move on this position, given enough information. Against this backdrop, how would high earners view income and wealth? Are their views malleable and might they be persuaded to think again about tax and the social programmes it pays for?

The Joseph Rowntree Foundation sponsored our research with additional assistance from the Barrow Cadbury Trust. In sessions conducted by Ipsos Mori over two evenings, we met partners in a law firm of international renown and senior staff in equally world-famous merchant banks. Their business is money, and they make it: the assembled law partners earned between £500,000 and £1.5 million, putting them in the top

Who do the super-rich think they are?

0.1% of earners in the UK. That may make them very high earners, but everything is relative: £1.5 million does not put them among the highest earners in their own firm. The silverbacks of the City law jungle earn up to £5 million a year. Our bankers were spread across a wider range of annual income, from £150,000 up to £10 million. Ipsos Mori have combined the results and the comments made by participants from both focus groups, though they met on separate occasions, one at Canary Wharf, the other in the City of London.

Before we began, participants were given questionnaires to tease out what they already knew about earnings. The questions came from British Social Attitudes (BSA), the big annual survey conducted by the National Centre for Social Research, which links answers to respondents' incomes. The most recent survey was taken in 2005, and examined the views of the top 10% of earners. Tom Sefton of the London School of Economics compared replies from our group with this wider evidence.

At first we probed factual knowledge about other people's earnings. We listed jobs: what did a factory worker or a cabinet minister earn, what should they earn? Are large income differences necessary incentives leading to national prosperity; are benefits too generous; should governments redistribute more? Next Professor John Hills, director of the Centre for the Analysis of Social Exclusion at the London School of Economics, presented the groups with facts about earnings – we reckoned that if the information came from a renowned economist it would be more credible.

The exercise turned into a startling demonstration of these City panjandrums' ignorance. Here were professionals who deal daily with money, yet how little they turned out to know about other people's incomes. When asked to relate themselves to the rest of the population, these high earners utterly misjudged the magnitude of their privilege. Gasps and even some blushing embarrassment greeted John Hills' demonstration of how wildly out they were over their own place in society.

People tend to imagine they are nearer the middle than they are. BSA shows that under half of those with earnings in the top 10% identify themselves as top people. Similarly those at the bottom of the scale put themselves nearer the middle too. We seem to have fond illusions about how alike we are: because we know someone richer and someone poorer we imagine ourselves middling, and on the back of such self-adjustment the UK deceives itself about unfairness. We do not even know how much close friends and relatives are paid.[2] But if myopia is a common condition, the high earners of Canary Wharf turned out to be as blind as bats. They knew less about earnings than the general public and were less accurate than the top 10% of earners in the BSA survey. Our bankers and lawyers were all comfortably in the top 1% of earners, yet here they were saying that 6% of earners were better off than them. They earned £150,000 plus, yet placed themselves on the scale below those actually earning £50,000 (pre-tax). One even placed himself plum in the middle, imagining 50% earned more than him – when the middle or median earnings, the halfway point at which half of full-time earners in the UK get paid more and half less, were £23,764 pre-tax in April 2007. They wanted to compare themselves with richer people, inventing a society in which they are a step or two down from the top. Comparing themselves upwards not downwards, they considered themselves normal, when they were anything but.

A high income in 2007 was £39,825, the sum it took to put an earner into the top tax band. Some 90% of the UK's 31.6 million taxpayers earned less than that, a fiscal fact our group found hard to believe. They over-estimated by four times what it takes to enter that top 10% bracket of earners in the UK: they thought it was £162,000. The BSA found the public at large get high income right, pitching it around that top tax-band threshold. It seems the more you earn, the more you miscalculate both high and low. In the BSA results, the top tenth of earners also misjudged it, estimating that high incomes begin at £52,000 a year – but that was still much closer to reality than guessed by our focus groups.

Our lawyers and bankers were next asked what they saw as the poverty threshold. They fixed it at £22,000. But that sum was just under gross median earnings, which meant they regarded ordinary earnings as poverty pay. Others have a surer grasp of who gets what. In 2004–5 (when the BSA last asked), a sample of the general public regarded £11,000 and under as low income. This was pretty much in line with official definitions: as of spring 2008, the poverty line for a childless couple was £11,284. Our bankers and lawyers thought a skilled factory worker earned £27,000 a year, well above the correct figure of £20,000; they exaggerated their own ordinariness by imagining others are paid more than they are.

Social imagining gets more accurate when people are asked to estimate earnings closer to their own grade. Our groups were more accurate on what professionals and other business executives earn, while the general population starts to go wrong at these upper levels, under-estimating what top people are paid. Our groups said a plc chairman would earn £653,000, three times the general public's estimate. That is broadly right, though as our group well knew, share options, pensions and bonuses are not included in that official salary figure.

Knowledge gaps like these should disqualify the wealthy from pontificating about taxation or redistribution. Financial ignorance matters because City views carry weight with ministers and politicians of all parties. Money men and women ostensibly speak with economic authority yet their social opinions deserve no more regard than those you might pick up in the street – maybe less. After John Hills had put up slides showing the right figures, one youngish banker said sheepishly: 'My appreciation of the numbers was quite hopeless. Given my age and my level of experience in the City I wouldn't have thought that I would be so out of touch with reality.' Another realized how much he had lost touch: 'It sounds an awful thing to say but I know people I went to school with, and I've no idea how they survive on the incomes they have.' But they got over their initial embarrassment quickly enough. An encounter with the facts didn't seem to impinge in the ensuing discussion; in no time they reverted to an under-informed view of the world.

Justifying their own high incomes, they reached for several arguments. It's not us, it's globalization, and anyway we are the nation's economic benefactors. 'The goose that lays the golden egg is the people who come to London to make wealth,' one said, echoed by all. The growing gap between rich and poor is 'a reflection of the success of policies here . . . making the City one of the pre-eminent financial centres of the world'. Another said defiantly, 'I don't think we should sit here and say London should be guilty for being successful.' They put themselves inside a golden enclave, but one on which the entire UK depended for its well-being. Don't mess with its denizens; they deserve thanks for providing invisible exports and powering GDP growth. We high earners belong to a global elite, able to work anywhere, always mobile.

Financial services are significant UK exporters, though the City of London's proportionate size is prone to exaggeration. Finance, including the City, insurance and high street banks, forms 7.9% of UK GDP compared with manufacturing at 14.7% and property services at 16.5%. Added together, hotel, catering and telecoms combine to nearly the same share of GDP as finance. As for their threats of flight, both our bankers and lawyers turned out to be remarkably immobile, most having worked for their firms for a long number of years. The warmth with which they described their London lives with partners and children suggested they would be loath to leave.

'We work harder and aspire the most.' Our groups thought themselves deserving because they worked hard and put in long hours. The longer we talked, the more they turned to moral reasons for success and failure, moving away from the structural globalization reasons given above. One banker said, 'It's a fact of modern life that there is disparity and "is it fair or unfair?" is not a valid question. It's just the way it is and you have to get on with it. People say it's unfair when they don't do anything to change their circumstances.' In other words, they see themselves as makers of their own fortune. Or as another banker said, 'Quite a lot of people have done well who want to achieve, and quite a lot of people haven't done well because they don't want to achieve; they're not in that environment which encourages opportunity.' One middle-aged woman banker described escaping from a provincial town where the main employer was the public sector: 'If you aspire to anything beyond that you're not going to live [there] any more, and that's the choice you make.' They had chosen a life that would make them rich while others, making different and morally equivalent choices, had abdicated their right to complain. 'Some of these are vocational, things like nurses . . . It's accepted, they go into it knowing that that's part of the deal.' And yet their self-exculpations were oddly impersonal, as if they were being swept along by a tide. Instead of confidently saying 'I'm worth it', they talked as if they just happened to be on the right side of history. It's a peculiar inversion of the tale of charismatic corporate leaders whose earnings reflect the unique qualities they bring to their companies.

Another said, 'Many people, like teachers, don't do things for the pay. But you won't find a teacher that works as hard as we do.' This was categorical, evidence unnecessary. They spoke of heroic all-nighters drawing up contracts for clients in time zones on the other side of the globe, a Herculean effort that justified fat pay. But did they work ten times as hard as a teacher on £30,000 a year or, in the case of some lawyers and bankers, a hundred times as hard? Such disproportionality did not enter their scheme of things; it wasn't for them to concern themselves with relativities. Nor did the high-flying lawyers quiz the relationship between their individual output and their firm's, which was odd since their pay depended also on how well their colleagues were performing.

Who do the super-rich think they are?

They certainly were silent on whether their mega-rewards stemmed from the peculiarly uncompetitive market in which a law firm operates. In economics textbooks, persistent high earnings should expand the supply of firms and attract new entrants into the market, forcing rewards down. This doesn't happen. These lawyers (and to some extent the bankers) receive the surplus returns that come from occupying a particular position and stopping others dislodging them. A cartel of prestigious law firms hogs the work, charging more or less the same. Restrictive practices of many kinds stop Tom, Dick or Harriet drawing up global contracts or doing commercial conveyancing cheaper – but that doesn't stop these lawyers using the language of markets and competition.

Nor does it change their view that for each of them personally their income is a matter of merit, or merit plus willpower. 'As long as you are aiming for it, the top jobs in the City are something that anyone can achieve,' one said. What's striking is not just the sociological naivety of that belief, but the lack of economic logic it displays. If everyone competed for top jobs, rewards should be driven down. Lawyers seemed more sociologically aware than the bankers and some acknowledged that family background made a great difference. Luck explained a part of their success and others' failure. One summed up: 'It's a bit of unfairness, a bit of ability, a bit of opportunity.'

In their view everyone benefits from high growth, including the poor; thanks to growth (which they claim to propel) everyone is a winner, everyone is better off. A lawyer said: 'It's just that there are different degrees of winner, isn't it? There are some people winning more than others.' Another said:

'Somebody who comes in a bottom 1% of the race may take a small booby prize, they're a loser in the division pie. But they're still better off than the equivalent person ten years ago.' They had already seen John Hills' tables showing what had happened to relative rewards in recent decades, with the concentration of high earnings for a few and the growing social gap, yet these relativities did not matter – except, of course, in their own firm or bank, where they were intensely conscious of even small differences in remuneration.

Wealth doesn't trickle down. These days even the Conservatives, using another watery metaphor, admit they were wrong to pretend a rising tide raises all boats. Money has to be directly channelled to the least well off and to services designed for them. Simply assuming that growth will sooner or later end up, albeit partially, in the pockets of the poor ignores the social damage caused by growing inequality. As for the argument that mitigating inequality would hurt growth, no one, especially our high earners, knows where the trade-off might start. A hard truth is that the interests of those at the top and those at the bottom are not the same.

The final justification for high pay used by our groups involved denial. None of us likes to feel guilty about our comfortable lives and it would have been absurd to expect mea culpas from these people just because they earned so much. What we had hoped for was more awareness, some recognition that their position needed explaining and even justification. Instead, with the exception of a couple of progressive lawyers, they simply denied they were rich. They could scarcely deny they had money, indeed they spoke of the pleasures that high incomes bought. 'I do enjoy the fact I can have nice holidays and don't think twice about buying particular items,' said one lawyer. Most simply blocked out the suggestion they were extremely well off. The rich, after all, are rarely cultural heroes. Getting to heaven is as likely as the camel navigating the eye of a needle. Few positive self-images are available to the wealthy. The Norwegian sociologist Stein Ringen argues in *What Democracy is For* (2007) that even though their power has expanded, the rich don't like to be put on the defensive over the legitimacy or size of their holdings. They like, he says, to conserve their 'moral capital', which would be depleted if they had to repulse convincing arguments for redistributive taxation.

Eschewing philosophy, our groups bluntly said they needed the cash. Living in London cost a lot: the city that made them rich was a reason you had to be rich. You had to afford London property. 'I'm sick of this, because with £100,000 in Manchester you are well off; £100,000 is a not a wealthy person down here.' A lawyer admitted that he couldn't imagine surviving on an income as low as £100,000, and in discussions about higher tax bands his colleagues objected to any such low sum being used as a benchmark. One of the more imaginative lawyers described their social isolation: 'We now live in a separate economy, we live on a separate level to the vast majority of people in the country. We don't send our kids to the same schools, we have more choice over schools, we have more choice over health, we have more choice over where we live, we have more choice over where we go on holiday and what we do for our jobs. And we live in a completely different world to the people we live next door to.'

London's divisions sat alongside their belief in super-London, the world city; they talked about belonging to it with pride and pleasure. Like other well-off people in London, they exult in soaring property values. They love the buzz of being the most affluent group in the city, going to the opera in Holland Park and watching the rugby at Twickenham. Here, of course, was another potent reason to doubt the argument that if they earned less or were taxed more they would flee.

At this point we naively suggested that money might just signal rank. Bankers could be paid in beans, as long as the biggest boys still got the most. What they paid in tax might not matter to them as much as boasting about the headline rate of their pre-tax packages? 'Don't kid yourself,' one of the lawyers responded with a smirk. 'It's not the status it gives you or where you are in the pecking order, it's the actual dosh in hand.'

Providing for children was flourished as a trump card, as if spending on offspring were automatically moral and good, regardless of how other people's children fare. 'I'm coming to work, I work hard, I've got two boys and I want to provide for them.' Providing for children meant buying them access to high earning jobs, taking trusted routes through school and university. One result of such social selection is already being seen on the City's doorstep. Applicants at this law firm are 'becoming posher', a senior partner noted. Older partners of this law firm were often grammar school but now recruits almost exclusively have been to private schools. They are also greedier: the same older partner said he was shocked that the first question high-flying graduates ask now is about the salary.

Our conversation turned to tax. High earners' arguments

against rebalancing the tax system ranged from threat to bluster to attack. Response one: we will leave, and you will be poorer. Or: we don't deserve to be forced to pay more. Or: even if we were taxed more, the money would all be wasted. John Hills' charts had shown how the modern UK tax system can barely be called progressive, with the top tenth of income earners paying a smaller proportion of their total income in tax than the bottom tenth. The poor are hit hard by VAT and other indirect taxes: they spent relatively more on taxable goods and services. Even when confronted with that evidence, the bankers especially gave the crudest response, saying flatly that they contributed more in cash – denying the point of a progressive tax system, which is that higher earners pay a larger proportionate share.

'Politics of envy!' one lawyer exploded furiously. 'I really object because what it does is take the whole emphasis and focus away into something that's totally irrelevant and won't help a poor person at all.' The idea of redistributing more was, he said, 'all kinds of bullshit crap which doesn't help the people!'. They felt a passionate hatred of capital gains tax and inheritance tax.

One banker, bearing a distinct resemblance to Mr Scrooge, said 'People don't starve in this country, it's OK. Compared with other countries, here you don't go hungry because you can just go and get money for free, right.' Some thought benefits already too high. One banker said he thought a family of four receives 'say, £3,000 a month in their hands, and they're somewhere miles up north. They're not going to earn that sort of money, so where's the incentive for them to go out to work?' In fact a family of four would in 2008 receive a net total of £1,328 a month.

Whatever, the poor didn't deserve it. Masters of the universe our groups might be but their outlook was pure *Daily Mail*: 'Single people . . . get pregnant and get a flat and more money. You just see everybody pushing prams, then they'll get more income and a little flat that they can stay in for life.' Another banker added, 'Take the youth of the last ten years, who have come out of single-parent families or families who have created a desire not to want to achieve.' There was much talk of the perverse incentives for single parenthood, with one banker complaining that the eighteen-year-old mother on benefit 'doesn't get that much less money than another eighteen-year-old working in a shop'. It didn't seem to occur to this speaker that the shop worker's pay might also be too low. They were contemptuous of anything that gave extra money directly to poorer people: 'This thing of giving pregnant women £200 for dietary supplements. Like, as if they'll really spend it on fruit.' Most were adamant, along with this banker: 'We don't think just chucking money at the welfare state is the answer.'

A last defence against paying more tax was their absolute conviction that government is inefficient and could not to be trusted with a penny more. 'Lack of ability is the main basis on which you get a job [in government],' said one lawyer. 'Nobody in the public sector is actually trained to do the job that they're required to do.' Another argued: 'Labour did a bit of that, with extra taxes and windfall taxes and the famous raid on pensions. The big debate is about how effectively all that money-raising has been applied. Most people would say not all of it was well applied.' We heard this get-out time and again, based on a doctrine spread daily in the press. Public money is always misspent. Our bankers airily said the administrative cost of paying tax credits was astronomical; John Hills said it was actually 3%. And what was the ratio of office costs to turnover in a big City bank? A good deal more, nearer 8% it turned out. But their ignorance was delivered with all the aplomb of power. What struck us wasn't just the contemptuous tone, but what their answers said about social interaction in modern London, perhaps in the country at large. These bankers and lawyers reported little or no social or professional contact with public officials of any seniority. Their views were based on hearsay, or occasional dealings with receptionists or call centres.

The entire public realm was dismissed in one sweep. As if he hailed from the planet Zog, one of the bankers said, 'I have absolutely no idea how my taxes are spent and therefore I do not trust the system at all.' But he knew his taxes would be misspent. 'The classic is how much you pay in your taxation versus what's invested in the roads and the transport system. It goes into a black hole.' A lawyer said, 'The problem we've got at the moment is the people who set targets and monitor delivery haven't got the faintest idea what they're doing.' One banker asserted that there is 'little accountability and measurability in the way that tax is actually used'. At this stage in the lawyers' group several of them swivelled in their chairs to point down river from their window to where the Millennium Dome floats like a jellyfish on its spit of land. 'Doesn't that', they cried in triumph, 'say all we need to say about the waste and futility of public spending?'

Here are people who may be technically adept, or good at deal-making, but as a group – with one or two exceptions – they were less intelligent, less intellectually inquisitive, less knowledgeable and, despite their good schools, less broadly educated than high-flyers in other professions. With minds this coarse, they wouldn't succeed in the higher ranks of the civil service, as heads of hospital trusts or good comprehensives, nor would they match up to the level of many junior ministers. Their high salaries were not a sign of any obvious superiority. Most dismaying was their lack of empathy and their unwillingness to contemplate other, less luxurious lives. They could not see that the pleasure they derived from possessions, prospects and doing well by their children is universal and that others deserve a share of that, too.

CHAPTER 2

The companies they keep

On 20 July 2007 the suite of halls inside the Queen Elizabeth II conference centre opposite Westminster Abbey hosted the annual general meeting of Cable & Wireless plc (C&W). The day's agenda was narrow. Shareholders alone – not customers, suppliers and certainly not staff – were allowed to speak. Their Zimmer frames and walking sticks marked them out as the old and retired, the usual suspects at AGMs. They are the small shareholders who own a tiny part of the communication giant's equity, the little people of the corporate world. Noses pressed against the window, today's meeting afforded them a glimpse of the executives who now pay themselves so much.

We're here because, in theory, shareholders can check and balance the boardrooms. The lawyers and the merchant bankers we heard from in the previous chapter were in partnerships; they wrote their own cheques. But it's through public companies that the ranks of the super-rich have expanded. Board decisions in plcs affect more than a single company. If they are profligate on pay, it will have a cultural impact, signalling merit and status in the social mainstream. Remuneration committees which fix boardroom pay and bonuses create the silverbacks of the economic jungle.

Although C&W is called a public company, its inner life is private. Decisions made by plc boards are closely guarded, even from staff, especially who gets what and why. The AGM, as J. K. Galbraith observed, is modern society's most elaborate exercise in popular illusion.[1] Despite the paraphernalia of votes and meetings, companies are not governed: instead they are the fiefdoms of managers, who align their own interests with the demands of the traders and intermediaries who profit from movements in the price of shares. The owners are the banks and pension funds which ostensibly have an interest in controlling corporate boardrooms. But because these funds are run by managers with a parallel interest in pumping up top pay, these would-be watchdogs barely yap at corporate salaries. They watch one another ratcheting pay up.

This meeting was conducted with exaggerated politeness. Directors were patronizingly gracious when the shareholders were ushered into the conference hall. Today's AGM had been billed as a shareholder rebellion. Here was a company steeped in British political history: founded in 1869, it was first to link imperial London to Bombay with undersea cables, was nationalized by Labour in 1947 and privatized by Mrs Thatcher in 1981. Legions of the Sids and Freds – who appeared on the advertising posters selling off these state-owned enterprises when Mrs Thatcher's ministers dreamt briefly of a 'people's capitalism' – were supposed to speak out. They were meant to rattle their pitchforks against the enormous bonuses the chairman, chief executive and others were awarding themselves; to fight against the C&W proposal to remove any cap on the amounts they could be paid.

Marie Antoinette would have blushed at the size of the cake being sliced up. Executives would get bonuses if the share price reached a certain point by 2010: the company's UK chief executive, John Pluthero, and its international chief, Harris Jones, would each receive £20 million on top of their salaries. But the board now argued that C&W's valuation in the equity markets was rising fast and might reach the magic marker before 2010. There was a danger that these upstanding managers would then sit on their hands, doing nothing much in the absence of a further cash incentive.

Pray silence for a moment of social-psychological reflection. What a narrow model of behaviour is on parade here. Imagine if workers had to be bribed with extra cash just to carry out their contractual responsibilities. Jobseeker's Allowance would be raised and raised again in order to make the people getting it strive harder to find work. Hospital cleaners would be paid a bit more every week, to make them scrub harder. But in the real world the logic of low pay runs in the opposite direction. At the poor end, benefits are cut to encourage more endeavour in job-seeking; cleaners' pay is kept low to clock up higher productivity per pound spent on the NHS.

C&W's non-executive chairman, Richard Lapthorne, was also demanding more. In defiance of corporate governance conventions, he wanted £11 million to keep his payment proportionate to the executives'. But if non-executives' pay is calculated on the same basis as managers', they soon stop being supervisors on behalf of shareholders and become cheerleaders for the executives – which is the story behind the boom in unjust rewards.

On the elegantly lit platform, C&W directors filed in to take their places at high table. They introduced themselves and their occupations, exposing as they did so their multiple directorships: Lapthorne also chaired Morse plc, the management consultants, and the New Look Group, the fashion business sold to private equity in 2007. Surprise, surprise, in February 2008 he was succeeded as chair of Morse by a fellow member of C&W's board. This crocheted pattern of mutual self-interest helps explains why no one blows the whistle on top pay. You sit on my board and I sit on yours; your chief executive doubles up as non-executive here and mine there; in the mix are the managers of banks and funds who control the shareholders' votes. Business talk is fiercely competitive; behaviour is cosier; markets and the companies operating in them are chummy. You scratch my back and . . . Pay packets at the top move in miraculously close formation; if the collaboration is not overt, it's an amazing coincidence how companies push salaries up by the same amount.

Next came presentations of C&W's results for the past year. The graphs headed impressively northward, especially the share price. What a wonderful job they are doing. The board exuded smugness: here was PowerPoint proof that their pay packages ought to rise too. 'The City loves this incentive programme,' chairman Lapthorne grinned. 'It is creating value and outstanding performance and they want to invest in companies that add value for them.' But what remarkably tight causality: paying Lapthorne millions equals profitability. What about the benchmarks, downplayed in the slides? How far was C&W from the (rising) market average?

When, finally, the little people got their turn, they picked up on this point. First on his feet was a well-known AGM attendee, John Farmer. A tall man in his late sixties, he owns shares in most FTSE 100 companies and scrutinizes their progress. The others turned to him as their champion as he launched the attack. Over five years C&W had just outperformed the index of telecoms stocks but under-performed in relation to the FTSE top hundred companies. 'This patchy performance is not a justification for a private equity-style remuneration,' he boomed. The pay package was repellent and contrary to the code of conduct for company boards agreed by the Stock Exchange. As for incentives: 'No one is indispensable. Others will work for this reasonable remuneration.' He sat down to polite cheers from half the auditorium.

Mr Chairman was placatory. Some might regard C&W's targets as unchallenging, but he certainly didn't. 'We're here for you, we're not here for ourselves,' Lapthorne said. Modest cough. 'I am paid in line with my peer group. I am here to add value. I don't feel it's fat-cattish. It's hard work.' Other shareholders stood up, rambled a bit, raising pernickety details from the annual report. One objected that the company's UK chief executive had not had the courtesy to appear before his shareholders properly dressed. John Pluthero had neglected to wear a tie, opting for a cool open-necked linen shirt master-of-the-universe look that did indeed subtly imply that only little people fussed about either ties or pay cheques.

After less than two hours, the AGM wound up. An effort had been made, but the pension-fund managers controlling most shares are usually passive, nodding through boardroom decisions on pay. On this occasion, one of their trade bodies, the Association of British Insurers, had flashed an amber warning over the C&W remuneration. Pensions Investment Research Consultants (PIRC) had recommended shareholders abstain from voting for the chairman's re-election in protest at the plan to award himself 5.5 million free shares. Abstention, in these circles, is as near as it gets to a vote of no confidence. But the institutional shareholders did nothing; profits were coming through so why bother with directors' pay? Lapthorne controlled millions of proxy votes already and so the board got its pay scheme through, no problem. It was a telling moment, when yet again shareholder democracy failed to address unjust rewards. Like the UK during recent times, companies have favoured the interests of those at the top. If we are after some self-correcting mechanism within business to end the pay bonanza, corporate AGMs are not it.

The shareholders shuffled into the foyer for a buffet lunch as a company flak whispered to us, 'The old dears only come here for the meal, you know.' As invigilation of a plc by its owners, this was a charade. Look what happened to Northern Rock: the board ended the worst year in its history, nationalization pending, by paying its chief executive a salary of £760,000 pro rata till he departed plus a bonus of £660,000 (*Financial Times*,

29/3/08). That's how effective boards are. However doughty and well-informed, elderly shareholders were never going to roil the deep pool of corporate complacency.

Lapthorne and Pluthero are fat cats whose excessive salaries prompt some to mount the pulpit. Savonarola, the rebellious fifteenth-century Florentine preacher, would have fun with the City of London during the twenty-first-century boom. But the problem is not directors' moral failing, an individual condition to be cured by a home visit from bishop or rabbi to administer a shot of spiritual correction. Boardroom excess, contorting income and wealth distribution, is a collective virus that not only infects the way business operates but ripples out into the assumptions and judgements made in society at large.

Pay for top executives has been rising by many multiples more than average pay. The *Guardian* and Reward Technology Forum survey (*Guardian*, 29/8/07) found that in 2006–7 chief executives' pay in the FTSE 100 companies soared by 37% over the previous year. In that year national average pay increased by 4% while the chancellor, Gordon Brown, insisted that public-sector pay increases be held at 2%. This vast percentage increase in top pay was no freak occurrence. In 2005–6 chief executive pay advanced 28%; the previous year it rose 16% and the year before that 13%. Between 2000 and 2007 FTSE top 100 chief executive pay grew 150% while median earnings across the whole population grew by just 30%.

To the top pay average of £737,000 in 2007, add bonuses, pensions and share options, which Income Data Services says took total average earnings up to £3.2 million – and that excludes the value of chauffeurs, meals and jets. Top of the league was the aptly named Bob Diamond, head of the investment arm of Barclays Bank, who earned £80 million. His pay was recommended by the ubiquitous Towers Perrin; this remuneration consultancy devised pay schemes for 44 of the 106 companies that featured in the FTSE 100. Corporate rewards, says Steven Tatton of Income Data Services, are being Americanized. In 1980 the average US chief executive earned forty-two times as much as the average manual worker. By 2000 he was earning 531 times the wages of a blue-collar worker, and 660 times in 2007.

If asked why they are paid so much, the Institute of Directors says 'exceptional performance should be rewarded' or, in the words of the L'Oréal ads, 'because I'm worth it'. But these rewards are incommensurable: they don't fit on any known scale. No calculus exists that justifies Diamond's £80 million as a measure of his performance, let alone relates it to the £18,000 paid to the security guard at Barclays' front door. That comparison is naive, the marketeers will say: Barclays profits for 2007 were £7.1 billion, making Diamond's pay an irrelevance in the company's accounts. So should top managers be classified as lucky jackpot winners or shamans, conjuring financial miracles? Nassim Nicholas Talib, in *Fooled by Randomness* (2007), argues that chief executives 'take a small number of large decisions, like the person walking into the casino with a single million-dollar bet. The link between the skill of the chief executive and the results of the company are tenuous . . . some of them are bound to make "the right decision".'

Top pay is said to be irrelevant to the bottom line, to the wealth of shareholders and the wealth of the company. Lord Browne, chief executive of BP, might have made £5 million a year out of its £12 billion turnover but if he had received £10 million it wouldn't have made a difference to the share price. But was Browne uniquely fitted for the job? Was he about to be lured away? How far did BP's share price depend both on market-wide movements (in the international price of oil for example) and on long-run strategies which by their nature were in place before Browne took the top job? The answers to each are highly ambiguous if not indeterminate.

Morality aside, high rewards are not causally linked to corporate effectiveness. Excess pay eventually becomes visible to those lower down and breeds organizational discontent. John Philpott, the chief economist at the Chartered Institute of Personnel and Development, talks of the need for 'a closer association between the way that organizations approach executive reward and reward strategy as applied to the rest of the workforce' – which put in ordinary language means fairness. A 2007 survey of human-resources professionals found that nearly all thought over-paying executives led to poor employee relations. Once ratios between top and lower pay levels shift too far, employees feel the workplace to be unfair and this perception harms an organization's effectiveness. The tolerable ratio seems to be inside 14 to 1. Managers set an example in their psychological contract with their staff: large pay differentials demotivate and demoralize. How enthusiastic did Tesco check-out staff feel to read that their boss, Sir Terry Leahy, earned 400 times their wage? How loyal did the bar staff of Punch Taverns feel when they read their boss Giles Thorley earned 1,148 times their minimum wages?

Super increases could be justified if (a) we could pin responsibility for success on individuals, like a medal on the breast of a war hero; and (b) those big numbers showed up elsewhere. But during these buoyant years for UK plc, the economy was growing at a trend rate of 2% to 2.5%, and much of that growth was down to consumption and extra public spending rather than the investment decisions of corporate chieftains. The FTSE 100 index rose in the 1990s, doubling between 1995 and 2000, losing nearly half its value to 2003 and then taking till May 2007 to recover its dotcom boom level. During all this time, average boardroom remuneration went in one direction, up. The gyrations of the index had a peculiar non-relationship with boardroom pay, especially in the down phases.

Vast, cumulating pay rises, with shares and pension entitlements on top, are not earned by superheroes, geniuses or by the exquisitely talented. They go to managers, few of whom are visionaries or rugged risk takers. For every Richard Branson there are a hundred business bureaucrats who are stewards, not creators of employment or new products or devisers of enduring corporate value. These managers make deals, cut costs and punt mergers in order to boost short-term share price. Where is the enterprise that justifies the heroic reward? If you put up your own money, venturing your argosy on the high seas, waiting anxiously on the quayside for its safe return, big rewards rightly follow. But managers are not risking their own cash. Boards now pay windfall gains for routine performance linked to general stock-market rises – and when bad decisions are exposed, as in the collective explosion of bad lending by banks, none ever had to repay the money they made for getting it wrong. Others paid for their mistakes.

Pay increases are often the result of a fix. They are pushed by consultancies with an interest in disproportionate rises. Two specialists, Towers Perrin and Kepler Associates, advise ten of the fifteen companies with the highest-paid executives. They tell remuneration committees that chief executive X should be compared with Y, whose pay they have also advised on. Gentlemen, wouldn't it be bad for your company's standing to deny him the same increments? Pay ratchets up. In the US it is called the Lake Wobegon effect, after Garrison Keillor joked that 'all the children there are just above average'. That's daft, since an average is just a way of describing a distribution; some observations, whether we are talking about income or height, will be above and some below. Beware averages, counsel Michael Blastland and Andrew Dilnot: 'In everyday speech "average" is a word meaning low or disdained. Within incomes, however, the average is relatively high' – because it only takes one Bill Gates to push the average into the stratosphere.[2]

One explanation sometimes offered for pay extravagance is charisma: there is a quasi-religious feel to a lot of talk about corporate leadership. Instead of wrestling with the complex interactions of market environment and the details of particular products, company boards prefer paying a lot of money to a big man. Harvard Business School professor Rakesh Khurana is deeply sceptical about the relationship between chief executive and corporate outcomes, at least in the medium to long run: 'To be hired as chief executive officer in many large corporations today, an executive need not meet any rigorous standard of skills or performance but only be the right sort of person from the right sort of company.'[3] The market for top jobs is rigged. Khurana found competition is often restricted to a handful of individuals who are valued for their social attributes rather than their skills and experience. Candidates need to be seen as legitimate by external constituents, financial analysts and the business media. No wonder the pool is small: shortage is a self-fulfilling prophecy, a social fiction not an empirical reality, when reputation is preferred to knowledge of company or sector experience. If there is a shortage of talent – the conventional justification for mega-payments – it is because boards 'employ extremely limiting criteria to define the pool of eligible candidates'.

But are these high-flyers tightrope walkers: do they need a golden safety net in case they tumble? Nick Isles, in *The Risk Myth* (2006), demolished the contention that top jobs are inherently risky. Chief executives' tenure is not much less than the average 5.5 years for British men of working age. On departure chief executives fall with golden parachutes, and waft smoothly into other highly paid directorships. Turnover for FTSE 100 chief executives is 14% a year compared with 18% for company executives at large, so compensation worth millions is paid to people whose lives are not high-risk. Compare their fate with that of the average employee who, when made redundant, stays out of work for fifteen weeks; one in five is still unemployed six months later. Not so the fourteen FTSE chief executives who moved jobs in 2006, only one of whom was made redundant, that bitter pill sweetened by a pay-off worth £5 million.

Another excuse is globalization. But Isles found that 86% of FTSE chief executives come from the UK, another 6% from within the EU (several from the Republic of Ireland) and only

8% from the US and the rest of the world. Most companies do not even recruit their chiefs from outside their own organization. In this static environment, Isles concludes that 'paying such large and inflationary pay increases is a perversion of market principles. Growing pay inequality corrodes the basic concept of fair reward that underpins a thriving society – and may also damage the performance and long-term success of organizations as staff become cynical and disillusioned.' The era of excess began in the 1980s. The boards of newly privatized companies realized that they were free to pay themselves what they pleased, under minimal external scrutiny. Cedric Brown was the emblematic fat feline. Bred in the nationalized gas industry, at British Gas plc he helped himself to a 70% pay rise without any material change in his responsibilities or any great leap forward in performance. In the economic upswing that began in the 1990s, corporate over-indulgence spread and the reason was the same – insufficient checks, absence of political commentary, complacent company owners. Andy Green, chief executive of BT group strategy and operations, received £535,000 worth of shares in the summer of 2007, on top of a 10% rise in his main pay package of £1.1 million, with no performance conditions attached, in order to 'keep him'. In October it was announced he was leaving to become chief executive of LogicaCMG.

Boardroom pay is like plunder, you take what you can get away with. 'This is a winner-take-all environment,' said Richard Lambert, chief executive of the Confederation of British Industry (CBI press release, 14/2/07). This business body once did represent 'industry' but has in recent times become a sort of high-class public relations agency for City boardrooms. Even Lambert, who smothered the critical instincts he displayed in his earlier job as editor of the *Financial Times*, has come to accept that pay poses, as he gingerly put it, problems of 'perception'. But no need to worry, accountability and efficiency ultimately are going to be ensured by the market. If UK plcs get fat and sloppy, private equity will buy them out. Like a prairie blaze, the theorists say, mergers and acquisitions burn out inefficiency; entire boards can be swept away when a company changes hands.

Private equity does away with the shareholders, and the comic annual ritual of the AGM. If the decadence of corporate governance at C&W is part cause of the camel train being stretched to breaking point, why not welcome 'creative destruction' as capital funds buy up plcs and establish a tighter link between managers' pay and performance? Flooded with capital, equity funds stalked plc boardrooms during the go-go years of the economic cycle that came apart in 2007. But the takeover boom inflated rather than punctured the growth of top earnings. Private equity turned out to be sleight of hand: in the five largest transactions in 2005–6 the equity component was about a fifth of the deal; most of the rest of the capital needed to buy the companies was borrowed on the security of the victim's assets, requiring it to generate income to service the debt for years to come. Private equity deals mostly sell off a company's assets for the sake of a quick win. Even the CBI is worried by the fact that, in Lambert's words, 'companies more or less disappear out of sight when they pass into private equity ownership. We get few details about their financial performance or business strategies. Just about all we have is a feeling that their managers and investors are making lots of money, one way or another.'

As the boom years faltered in 2007–8, private equity retreated. Yet while private corporate ownership may ebb and flow with the willingness of banks to lend at what are now seen to have been dangerously low rates, the recent private equity phenomenon has reinforced the temptation for plc boards to pay themselves excessively. Private equity removes the last vestiges of public accountability that come with plc status. Forget about corporate social responsibility and irritating, if impotent, shareholders. Robert Peston's *Who Runs Britain?* (2008) confronted the argument that capitalist exuberance translates into aggregate welfare. 'The argument that the activities of hedge funds and private equity are somehow greatly to the benefit of the vast majority of us is for the birds. Their spoils are usually an opportunity lost to the pension funds on which most of us depend for our retirement income. The companies they either buy or boss around may sometimes be strengthened. But frequently they are reconstructed to generate massive short-term gains, with little positive long-term benefit. Worse still, private equity and hedge funds are a manifestation of the era of cheap money which has undoubtedly been a source of great harm to the economy.'

The CBI used to believe that plcs could be reformed. In 1990, following anger at high rewards during the recession and scandals over the collapse of the Bank of Credit and Commerce International and Polly Peck, directors were stirred into action. Sir Adrian Cadbury, chairman of Cadbury Schweppes, proposed a code of best practice for boards in 1992. Three years later, the chairman of Marks & Spencer, Sir Richard Greenbury, speaking for the CBI, said all boards should have audit and remuneration committees with non-executive directors. A further tightening of board procedures followed the 2003 report for the Department of Trade and Industry from Sir Derek Higgs, chairman of Alliance & Leicester, and the report for the Treasury by Paul Myners, another former chairman of Marks & Spencer, on the governance of pension funds. Labour made remuneration committees compulsory.

But better 'corporate governance' did not lead to better behaviour. Non-executives turned out to be more interested in fattening their own pay than scrutinizing the rewards of executives: median pay for a senior independent director in a big company was at least £30,000 a year in 2005, for a smallish time commitment. The *Guardian*/RCT survey found one in five of these part-time directors was paid £1 million in 2006–7 and many earn much more by sitting on several boards. The pitiful creature that shareholder democracy showed itself to be at the C&W AGM is part of the reason. In company legislation which came into force in 2007, Labour did seek to strengthen the arm of dissident shareholders, giving them extra rights to push and probe. It was a welcome step but it is unlikely to turn shareholders into a countervailing force – and so far has done nothing to check the upsurge. A High Pay Commission might help curb excesses, if it were to set benchmarks for top pay increases, with advisory guidelines that reflect rewards in the economy at large and establish some fairer ratio between top and bottom.

The companies they keep

We needed to hear from inside a mainstream boardroom and, to his credit, the chairman of J. Sainsbury plc, Sir Philip Hampton, was willing to talk. Hampton was once a top man at Lazards, the investment bank, then finance director of British Steel, British Gas, BT and Lloyds TSB. Thoroughly experienced in the world of finance and industry, he caught our eye because he has been a rare voice prepared to speak critically about the executive pay explosion. 'It's a big worry. If it does not stop we will see £4 million, £5 million or £6 million become the average' (*Sunday Telegraph*, 24/9/06). Having heard him speak with civilized intelligence at a think-tank event, we asked to meet.

Jagged examples of social dislocation were on display the day we talked. That morning the Treasury had instructed local councils in England to pay no more than 2% to their 1.3 million employees, though inflation was running at 3%. These workers are mostly the low paid, 75% of them women: care assistants, classroom assistants, cleaners and refuse collectors. On the same day UNICEF reported damningly on children's well-being. And, close to Hampton, news had just broken that piranhas from private equity were circling his company. Sainsbury's, a high street fixture, was about to be seized by brigands and broken up, its property portfolio ransacked. As it turned out, Hampton's complacency about the threat was justified – the assault on Sainsbury came as the private equity wave was cresting.

Hampton worked in a glass eyrie above Holborn Circus, paid £395,000 a year for his part-time post. Sainsbury's chief executive was then on £1.47 million. Hampton regarded his own remuneration almost as pocket money; he had earned a fortune long ago working in the City. 'For a long time now I haven't had to work to keep body and soul together,' he said. So how well off was he? 'Oh, I'm only worth millions, not many tens of millions.' He had one house in Surrey stockbroker country. 'My one mad expenditure is my yacht. But I haven't got a crew.' In every milieu there are fine gradations of status, so among yacht owners, not having your own crew is déclassé, like Michael Heseltine when Tory aristocrats sneered that he could afford to own a stately home but had to buy his own furniture.

Hampton's concern about pay is genuine. He dislikes the misleading language used to cover up excess. 'Basic pay' is a misnomer and bonuses are no such thing. 'If you look at FTSE 100 senior executives, routinely they are getting 70 to 100% of their basic pay again in bonuses. It's called a "target" bonus but the man in the street would call it basic pay. The same is true of share options. People find it helpful not to call it basic pay so it doesn't make such an appearance in the headlines. But you no longer have to do great work to get a great bonus. If you said to someone this year your bonus is zero, you might as well fire them. This is a big shift in the last five years. We've mangled the words in recent years and I don't think companies are being as straightforward as they should be. They should only pay out if the company does exceptionally well.'

What he wanted was transparency, not a brake on top pay. 'The driver is absolutely top talent, a relatively small number of people who have become more mobile. Take Justin King, our chief executive, an outstanding executive from Mars, Grand Met, Asda and M&S. Lots of companies would love to employ him and he could be paid more elsewhere.' Does one man make so much difference? If he fell under a Rolls-Royce wouldn't others as well qualified step up? No, Hampton said, especially in retail. King is credited with turning Sainsbury's around the way Stuart Rose turned round M&S. But Hampton admits the market for such talent isn't global. He too says pay inflation has been manufactured by the remuneration consultants who help set pay at the top. 'Pay is remorselessly benchmarked with big fat books about what everyone else has got and what's the median, the average, the top decile and the bottom quartile. It's almost implicit that it leads to a natural trading up. A statement that you are positioning yourself in the fourth quartile is a statement that you are happy to take, you know, fourth quartile people.' Hampton's point here makes little sense. In any distribution, there has to be a fourth quartile. Somebody, by definition, falls into it. But who said boardroom pay was rational?

This liberal-minded tycoon argued for transparency and for merit to be re-established as the main justification for boardroom pay. Although welcome, corporate reforms would only reshuffle the front runners in the camel train. What about the distance between them and the others? The note of disquiet sounded by Hampton is a hopeful sign of discontent. If the sheikhs are not as happy as their gaudy affluence might imply, perhaps they could be persuaded to look around at how the others are faring. They know boardroom excess is unsustainable, and it's not going to be cured by some slight correction in the markets, or even a recession.

CHAPTER 3

The discreet anxieties of the bourgeoisie

Hanover Square in London's West End was not always safely prosperous. In 1818 a Tory government decided the restless residents needed more spirituality, to stop them getting revolutionary ideas, so it paid for the construction of two fine churches in the vicinity, as part of a programme of assistance to the Anglicans. These days the square is full of commercial bustle, yet from one corner of a stylish magazine office there comes a distinct and unexpected whiff of social unrest.

Geordie Greig is doing a quick sum on the pad at his desk, trying to work out what an 'ordinary middle-class person' needs to get by in London these days. Greig's idea of ordinary is extraordinary. He is editor of the *Tatler*, connoisseur of Sloane chic, a bit-part player in the Diana drama and the self-appointed spokesman for the capital's traditional upper classes. For all its oddity, his cry of affluent angst is worth hearing.

The discreet anxieties of the bourgeoisie

We, the old English upper-middle classes, are being out-classed, he complains. Old money that used to enjoy its own circuit – Ascot, Henley, Eton's 4th of June – and the trappings of a certain style of life now finds itself displaced and outpriced. The sums on his notepad show private schooling for four children costs at least £50,000 a year. He scribbled on additional costs: a people carrier, family holidays, children who demand top brands and a walloping mortgage in the quadrants where anyone worth knowing would want to live, Notting Hill-ish perhaps. Add it all up and to get by, he reckons you wouldn't have much change from a £500,000 pre-tax income. To the real and pretend aristos who people the pages of *Tatler*, that once used to be serious money. But to London's multitudinous high-net-worth incomers, half a million is hardly a benchmark, and a far from impressive income.

Greig wrote a piece for *Tatler* in July 2007 that in any other publication might have been called class envy. It was a war cry by the ordinary rich against the super-rich. They feel they have been – to use a Marxist term they would once never have dreamt of applying to themselves – expropriated. 'London is being split in two by excessive amounts of cash and competit-iveness that have also turned our capital into a separate nation. [A] social earthquake is transforming the upper end of British society. The relentless rise of the super-rich has divided upper-income earners into two tribes: the have-a-lots and the stress-a-lots. London is more than paved in gold, it is coated in it. Never has there been such ostentatious display of wealth or such frenzied consumption.'

An odd complaint, you might think, coming from an old

Etonian whose commercial success depends on advertisements for multi-million-pound properties, £1,000-a-week nannies, £45-an-hour private tutors, Damien Hirst art objects and £16,000 Louis Vuitton handbags. He shrugs. 'There is a them-and-us divide between those from traditional British families who feel entitled to a privileged lifestyle and those who are buying into it and squeezing them out.'

So there is no love of globalization here in Hanover Square. Greig protests at an 'influx of clever, competitive foreigners who want our schools and houses', who pay little tax compared with the 'hard-working middle-class professionals, many of whom can no longer afford to pay school fees or buy nice houses in the places where they were brought up and which they consider home'. Now the upper classes are feeling the same anger at immigration as some of the working class, but immigrants of a much higher-earning sort. His resentment illuminates Labour's shilly-shallying over taxing non-doms; Greig and others are outraged that they should escape the taxes others pay, raising the price of property with access to loopholes allowing them to avoid paying capital gains tax on it.

Greig tells of a 'Dior-dressed American mother' of a four-year-old marching into an entrance interview at the Kensington Thomas's, one of a mini-chain of London prep schools, pushing ahead of the queuing parents and demanding to see the head-mistress. 'My daughter Malvina can speak five languages,' she announced. Malvina got in and the rueful witness's child did not. 'Welcome to pressure-cooker London,' says Greig. These pushy mega-rich infants are hot-housed from birth and, once professionally crammed, they sail into the schools of their choice.

The discreet anxieties of the bourgeoisie

When they do manage to get into the right schools, Greig complains that upper-middle-class children feel left out when the super-rich children can take half-term holiday breaks in Dubai costing £10,000.

On one level all this is risible. We are being invited to worry about distinctions between people who are in the top 0.1% of the income distribution. But these complaints tell us that economy and society in Britain have been torn. Inequality isn't just a story about the poor and dispossessed. It's not just about envy. Excess at the top hurts others. The penthouse apartment in the Richard Rogers Partnership development overlooking Hyde Park which was sold before it was built for £100 million – that's £53,821 per square metre – has a knock-on effect, spreading out through the national property market to first-time buyers far from Knightsbridge. The rips and tears in the fabric of society go all the way up and down the social scale, as top managers try to catch up with the boardroom and middle managers resent the gap above them opening up.

Ask the specialists who monitor what happens to pay up and down the social scale. Peter Christie, director of reward consulting at consultants the Hay Group, says 'There's no doubt at all that the stretch between the bottom and the top has affected differentials at all intermediate levels within companies and organizations. The differences between professionals and the functional heads in the middle have widened, as has the stretch between the functional heads and the heads of section, and between them and the chief executive. There's no doubt shop-floor roles have been held relatively in line with general earnings, while higher roles within a company have accelerated at a faster rate.' So everyone feels the stretch, wherever they are. In the camel train, even in the top *Tatler* ranks, it can be painful to see the sheikhs up ahead cantering unreachably faster than the rest.

Greig's bleat of pain echoes an old British lament about the decline of aristocratic authority and the death of deference – the theme of a book by Peregrine Worsthorne a few years ago (*In Defence of Aristocracy*, 2004). Old money has always resented the rise of the new. English landowners claiming an ancestry back to William the Conqueror (yet another usurper) bemoaned their fate even as they banked the cheques they got from selling their estates or marrying into trade. Upper-middle-class angst at finding themselves overtaken is hardly a pressing social problem but it is another interesting symptom of the widening gaps. No need to weep for them – but note the political potential for action. Those in the upper middle of the camel train also want restraints on wealth.

Greig's complaint is a hotchpotch of woes. He paints a picture of an old Etonian, proud survivor of the wall game, gazing mournfully into restaurant windows round the corner from where he was brought up, but no longer able to afford to eat, let alone live there. It's hardly incisive political analysis – he complains at paying £25 a day in people-carrier congestion charges without pausing to wonder whether he might take public transport. That is characteristic of the rich: of all the journeys made each year, the top tenth of the income distribution make the fewest on foot. Yet Greig presents himself as a recruit to the ranks of those alarmed by the growth of inequality. 'That old sense of living in a country where fair play and an honest day's work led people to feel they could get what they strove for has been destroyed by dizzying extremes in wealth.' We may laugh at his notion of fair play and an honest day's work. When did a cleaner or carer ever get either? But his anxiety shows that whoever you are, wherever you may be on the income scale, everyone has a sticking point where 'enough is enough', where the sight of the wealth gap yawns too wide. In his discomfort is political opportunity.

Greig does not agree the rich should pay higher taxes – unless, he muses, a new top tax band were set at incomes of £2 million or more. Governments always waste money, especially Labour, he adds predictably. Yet his shriek is a paradoxical condemnation of Labour for having let the top rip. The toffs or would-be toffs of *Tatler* are willing the Tories to say that exponential incomes are socially damaging, corrosive and destabilizing. David Cameron dipped his toe into this pool when he promised in October 2007 to tax 'non-domiciled' residents at a flat rate of £25,000 a year, using the £3.5 billion raised to finance his deep cuts in inheritance tax. This was a direct transfer from the astronomically rich to the Geordie Greig rich, showing he understood that upper-middle England doesn't think runaway under-taxed millions are fair.

Greig's views are reflected by those a bit lower on the income scale – by Middle England. It shares many of his anxieties. It too tends to think governments waste taxpayers' money, yet there is one big difference. Middle England thinks that the rich should pay more tax.[1] Their attitudes towards fairness change once they absorb information of the kind too often absent from daily reporting and debate. Once they hear how deprived are the lives of the one in three children in poverty, people do shift.

Suspicions about those drawing benefits soften. Most think the distribution of rewards should be fairer.

When the Fabian Society assembled a Middle England focus group to discuss child poverty, we sat in as observers.[2] Ipsos Mori selected participants from average middle-income voters, neither strongly left nor right in their politics. At first they expressed the typically British view that poverty is due to laziness and personal failings.

They thought no children were poor, but if they were, then bad parents were to blame or family size, alcohol or drugs. Any pity felt for children was erased by 'selfish parents who want to spend all their money on booze or going out'. Their conviction came not from personal experience, but almost exclusively from television and newspapers. The 'hard-working' were sharply divided from those on benefits, but the group had no notion that the majority of the poor work, and it's low wages that make them poor: the focus group was astonished to learn that 54% of people living below the poverty threshold are working.

After a couple of hours, attitudes were shifting. They heard that children brought up under the poverty line were three times more likely than average to die as babies, five times more likely to die in accidents, at higher risk of mental illness and destined to have shorter lives. What stirred them further were accounts of daily reality, children without warm coats, holidays, schools trips or birthday parties. No one had heard of Labour's pledge to abolish child poverty but were impressed to learn that over 600,000 children had been lifted out of poverty by 2005. They were taken with evidence that poor parents defied the stereotype and spent what they got in extra tax credits on their children.[3]

Debating among themselves, this focus group became animated. If it really works, then of course it should be done, they started to say. Bad parents, they now believed, made the case for government investment in better parenting schemes and education in the early years. Finally, a crunch question: how much would they be willing to pay? Nearly all settled on a 2p-in-the-pound increase in income tax, bringing in £7.2 billion a year – enough to provide a Sure Start children's centre in every neighbourhood as well as paying for cash benefits and credits to poor families that would go at least half the way to meeting the abolition-of-poverty ambition.

This was a deliberative group, with time to talk and learn. You can't take the whole population to a hotel for six hours to discuss child poverty – and a spasm of generosity in a focus group does not guarantee pro-tax votes in a polling booth. Yet the exercise showed that, once convinced about child poverty and how it can be alleviated, people will change their positions. Middle England retains a sense of natural fairness. But how to get past its suspicion of scroungers to tap that well of solidarity?

The political challenge is formidable, but as the growth of inequality makes people anxious it seems more possible; Middle England joins the upper-middle class and even a smattering of the top 1% of earners in registering unhappiness. The editor of *Tatler* may express it differently from the chairman of Sainsbury's, but their worries coincide over their children's debilitating affluence and social exclusion and the blunting of moral sensibility. Hampton echoed the American billionaire

Warren Buffet, who famously said he wanted to give his children enough so they could do anything, but not enough so they could do nothing.

Researching this book, we heard even the stridently assertive rich, so sure about their own right to earn and keep whatever they liked, grow diffident and uncertain over their children and how to stop them drifting into the empty lives of spoiled wasters. Rich parents wanted the one thing they could never give their children – the normality of belonging to and sharing in ordinary British life. It's a paradox in a society where community seems to be low on our list of priorities.

If rich parents feel queasy, so do some of those charged with educating their affluent offspring. Public schools are not altogether happy gardeners of plutocracy's seedbeds. Headteachers take umbrage at their pupils' lifestyles and expectations. Codes implying that the right behaviour is selfless behaviour tick faintly away; some schools still sing Kipling's hymn 'Non Nobis Domine', 'Not unto us, O Lord'. The Headmasters' and Headmistresses' Conference (HMC) represents 250 of the top private schools and annual meetings have lately rumbled with concern about their values. Perhaps a sign of their own drop in ethical standards was the Office of Fair Trading disclosing that top schools were colluding to fix fees – a dishonest and illegal practice. That their victims were ultra-rich doesn't exonerate the offence.

Largely invented in the Victorian era, the public-school ethos of playing for the team not the individual, of seeking the greater and not the personal good, was always self-deceiving, yet schools felt obliged to paint their pupils' inherited privilege with a gloss of duty to serve others. These days parents are buying rank and separation and guaranteed attainment: the Sutton Trust has found that the 7% of private-school children take 45% of Oxbridge places and these pupils are five times more likely than state-school leavers to be offered a place in a top Russell Group university. *Noblesse* no longer obliges. And these children are not aiming for leadership in the land, but for isolated money-making careers.

Outside the headmaster's study at The Perse, the Cambridge private school, the notice board is emblazoned with the school motto in Latin but it's not just the language which makes it anachronistic. *Qui facit per alium facit per se*: who serves others serves himself. Apparently an exhortation to do good to others, its ambiguity exquisitely captures the public schools' enlightened self-interest. Politics was once based on a lurking fear that if the upper classes didn't watch out, the plebs might rise up in revolution or clout them over the head with a cudgel outside their club and steal their wallet. Giving something back was a sort of social insurance policy that at least acknowledged that they all belonged to the same society. Public schools produced officers and gentlemen who would occasionally ride up and down the camel train to see everything in the nether ranks was shipshape: patronizing, undemocratic, unquestioning of their God-given superiority, they did at least belong.

The Perse, like other public schools, offers education to the affluent from age three through to the sixth form. Its grounds roll beautifully on the edge of the university city, and its well-appointed labs, halls, libraries and manicured lawn spell out that biblical promise – to those that have, more shall be given.

Once, ironically, it was called the Cambridge Free School. 'We have a selective intake,' says the school prospectus, 'and we assume that our pupils will proceed to the major universities.'

The headmaster, Nigel Richardson, retiring in 2008, is old-school, and the fact he himself was once head boy at Highgate indicates how closed this world can be for masters as well as parents. We spoke to him in his study overlooking the greens. At the time he was the chair of the HMC and evidently unhappy.

'It matters, the growing gap between rich and poor,' he said with a forthrightness that his impending retirement might have encouraged. 'I can see it storing up problems for these children in the future.' He fears a world in which the rich will live together, gated against the threatening semi-savages outside – he refers fearfully to a recent dystopic novel by P. D. James. Here at The Perse, 'the children have little inkling of where they stand in relation to others. They know they are academically successful, but they don't know they belong to a tiny elite. They are far more privileged than they realize. If they think about state schools, the one that probably comes to mind is the Ridings, the worst school trotted out by the press time and again.'

Richardson is disturbed by his charges' state of mind, alarmed at the nine-year-old who said he felt left out because he was the only boy in his class who had never been outside Europe on holiday. Our money-obsessed society dismayed him. 'It took off with the yuppie syndrome in the 1980s. We are becoming more selfish with less regard for others. Look at the decline in volunteering. You can't find anyone to be scoutmasters any more so I have to pay someone to do it as a job. Some of our pupils might do some teaching on gap years in Latin America or Africa, but most go off travelling instead. If I gave a school assembly and talked about "duty" I would struggle. I couldn't do it.

'I did try the other day to tell them off about the disgusting state they were leaving the changing rooms in for our cleaners to mop up after them. I said it was our responsibility to be grateful for our job prospects and very grateful that we would never have to do jobs like theirs.'

He knows he has vastly more to spend on each of his pupils than is available per child in comprehensives. He knows how many state-school pupils need extra spending on them in staff and equipment. Gordon Brown pledged that per capita spending on state secondary pupils would match that in the private sector, but when? R. H. Tawney called the system of educational selection by parental bank balance 'the hereditary curse upon English education', and the malediction is not about to be lifted any time soon.

For the privileged the dice are loaded ever more heavily. Top universities will continue to under-represent the majority of students whose parents don't or can't pay for their education. Richardson takes a deep breath and says, 'I don't think it can go on like this. I think we heads should get together and say enough is enough, it's time to intervene. We need higher taxation and we need to use the money to make society more equitable. How do you stop politicians promising more tax cuts, when we need more spent?' But how many Perse parents would warm to that sentiment?

'I'd like to bring heads together to say something like that, but what would my staff say about paying more tax, or my governors?' Compared to him, some of the new generation of public-school heads come across like company chief executives, pumping out ever higher exam results and not much interested in social justice. But the closer schools resemble commercial firms, the more problematic the relationship between the teachers and the taught. Go too far down the money road and you might as well sell A-levels.

For his part, Richardson treasured an article written by John Rae, the former head of Westminster School, in 1987. Called 'Tom Brown's Porsche days', it was his response to the City-fuelled Thatcher boom, then in full swing, and instigated by one of the school's former pupils, Nigel Lawson, the chancellor of the exchequer. Public schools, Rae said, had come to 'endorse the priorities of the age: every man for himself in the competition for good A-levels, a good university and a red Porsche to roar up the school drive, scattering your former teachers like nature's rejects in the race of life'.

Heads themselves were starting to speak 'of the old boy who is earning a six figure salary in much the same tones of awe and pride they once used for a fellowship at All Souls. They would like to invite a missionary to address the sixth form but they settle for a well-paid yuppie, because that way they can guarantee an audience. They preach the importance of service to the community, but they know it does not pay enough to interest their pupils. A handful of their boys will consider what used to be called a vocation or a career in public service. The brilliant scholar with a double first at Oxford is not going into the church; he's going to Harvard Business School.'

The discreet anxieties of the bourgeoisie

Not many will weep over a public-school head's crisis of confidence. These public-school heads can hardly be called closet egalitarians, since private schooling is a prime way of transmitting privilege. Labour's Charities Act 2006 said all charities must have stated aims for the 'public benefit' and principle 2c insists 'people in poverty must not be excluded from the opportunity to benefit'. Applied without qualification to the public schools, which have the status of charities, it would be revolutionary. In practice the public schools can stay within the law by offering free places to bright local children. The bonus would be a boost in their results from having skimmed the cream of local state-school pupils.

But Richardson at The Perse is registering something, just as in his cocksure way Geordie Greig is making a point about socio-economic trends. Can mega-money coexist with social order? What ordinary sense of social obligation guards against children who think money is all that matters, growing up to be crooked lawyers and dodgy bankers or, short of that, bankers who take a risk too far or lawyers who make a profession helping others to avoid every social duty, especially tax? In the long run extreme inequality will harm the princelings in these schools' care as well as the paupers at their gates. In 2007 a UK bank launched an assets and responsibility course for the children of the wealthy 'after realising that wealth can destroy motivation' (*Financial Times*, 23/2/08). There is something worrying happening in our society today and those at the front half of the camel train are aware of it too.

PART TWO

The Camel Train: The stragglers behind

CHAPTER 4

Alison tries to keep up

Renting a council house is a mark of Cain: in 2006, 35% of the heads of households in social housing were of working age but did not work. Even after their rents and housing benefits were taken care of, six out of ten of their children were deemed to exist below the official poverty line. Those who live in social housing – which we now euphemistically call renting from a council or housing association – belong to another world. In *Estates: An intimate history* (2007), Lynsey Hanley captures the closed, cut-off feel of where the poorest families live. London is exceptional insofar as the poor and high earners tend to live cheek-by-jowl, estates interleaved with expensive streets, physically close and yet worlds apart. The well off rarely step inside to look, instead falling back on the stereotypes of poverty supplied by the media. Reality TV offers up gargoyles and grotesques to gawp at, obese, multi-partnered, slattern and sloven. The Tories say there is a tide of dysfunction, equating 'dysfunction' with the one in seven UK births that are to women not living with the child's biological father.[1] More careful estimates based on such factors as income, health and employment suggest 2% (around 140,000) of UK families with children are 'multiply deprived'.[2] That 2% are the ones who would be regarded as having serious problems, yet they are the ones wrongly held up as typical of all poor families.

Ignore the labels. One mother and her children are struggling below the poverty line, yet they still aspire and dream of betterment. Their motivation and moral qualities are pretty much like many a better-off family's – the only difference is money.

They live in Kingstanding, a sprawling outer-city council estate, half an hour on the number 91 from the centre of Birmingham. The houses, pre-1945 low-rise terraced, mixed rented and right-to-buy purchased, are occupied mostly by white residents. The age of the houses and ethnic balance aside, Kingstanding is like hundreds of other estates where you can find the other end of the camel train. We are on our way to visit Alison Murray, a single parent with three children, to listen to her life story and ask: is it fair, is it wise, is it functional to allow such a wide gap to open up between her sons and the average?

The bus from the city centre is a lifeline since so many Kingstanding households are without a car. Of UK families 27% have no transport of their own – the same proportion as those who don't own their homes. As Mrs Thatcher is reputed to have said, travelling by bus is a sure sign of failure in anyone over the age of twenty-six.

Once, the social mix on council estates was leavened with the skilled and aspiring working classes, but they have upped and gone, buying their own homes elsewhere. Tenure is the index of social division: 4 million people in England live in social rented homes, many on estates which are demographically over-burdened with poor pensioners and poor children, with two thirds or more of total rent met from benefits. Although 54% of poor children live in a family where one parent does work, with only a third of working-age adults in a job, estates are increasingly places for the sick, the mentally ill, new migrants, single mothers and life's stragglers.[3]

However, people here do still inch forwards too, their standard of living improving with each generation. Children have shoes. Gone are the outside toilets attached to the back of Kingstanding houses: they have been reconstructed to open inwards into the ground floor near the kitchen. Television, DVD players and mobile phones are found in most households living at the poverty line and the council is gradually fitting central heating. Because the cost of electronic goods has plummeted – thanks to trade with China – the poor possess things that once were luxuries. Globalization creates wealth by bringing cheaper gadgets, yet the same global whirlwind sends hard-pressed families into debt on their energy and food bills and drives their pay below subsistence levels.

Almost 13 million people, about a fifth of the UK population, have household incomes below the official poverty line. Many voters are dubious, because they are reluctant to concede that poverty is a relative condition. But the hurt of being poor comes from lacking what others enjoy as everyday necessities. Stein Ringen says, in *What Democracy is For* (2007): 'It is about dignity, the ability to make choices and live one's own life, the risk to children, the feeling of exclusion.' Recognized by Adam Smith in the eighteenth century, the relative conception of poverty has struggled long and hard to win over the public, especially the public in England. If poverty is a relationship to what others (society at large) have, a threshold needs to be set. The Joseph Rowntree Foundation was due to publish a 'minimum income standard' in July 2008, based on extensive consultation with the public over what they thought were basic needs: these included not just food and shelter but enough resources to participate in society (having school-friends round for tea) and maintain dignity (dry-cleaning a suit).

The UK uses a poverty measure established by the United Nations and the Organisation for Economic Cooperation and Development (OECD) at 60% of the median income. So being poor is subsisting on two thirds of the general standard of living – half the people on less than the median income and half on more. Taking all UK households of the same kind together, including those where pensioners live and there are no earnings from work, the median 2008 income for a two-adult, no-children household (adjusted for housing costs to ensure comparability, and after tax and benefits are counted) was £18,824. Being poor meant living on 60% or £11,294, which is £217 week. For a single mother with two children, the 2008 poverty line was £260 a week, worked out on the basis of 60% of the median income for similar households, higher because of the benefits paid to children For a couple with two children, the threshold was £332 a week.

Alison tries to keep up

When in 1998 Labour pledged to abolish all child poverty it targeted the 3.4 million living below the poverty line, or 26% of all children. By 2005–6, on a like-for-like basis, the number was down by 600,000. Labour's 2010 target was to halve the figure to 1.7 million children, but few think it likely. A fifth of all UK children are still living in poverty in 2008. Labour's target entails channelling more money to poor households. Simple, as an objective; difficult politically. But to those who say it's utopian or socially naive or arithmetically impossible to attempt to abolish poverty, the response (once again) has to be – look at Scandinavia. It was accomplished, in Norway, in 2003.[4]

The press loves discovering the neighbours-from-hell family with ten children (preferably foreign in origin) whose benefits add up to gigantic sums, and the attitudes of our group of lawyers and bankers demonstrated how such mud sticks. Poor dysfunctional families from that bottom 2% make good copy, but everyday ordinary poverty is harder for others to recognize. Better-off people with cash to spare easily forget how households on tight weekly budgets are plunged into debt by extras such as rising energy bills, school uniforms or new shoes. Not being able to afford a newspaper, a drink or a bus fare is beyond the comprehension of most of us who are not poor. How can those poverty figures be telling the truth, people wonder, when everyone in their area looks shiny and prosperous – but it all depends on where they live. In Blackburn, 38% of the population are poor: 52,000 people in a town of 137,000. If that sounds too far away from the City, try Southwark, where 81,000 of 245,000 inhabitants are poor.[5] But social myopia blurs any accurate view of people not like us, even if they live nearby.

The Camel Train: The stragglers behind

Alison Murray is statistically typical of the 766,000 single mothers in the UK living on income support. Single mothers are much excoriated, yet hardly known. She is not wayward, deficient or hopeless, not one of those mothers with a score of children by different men, not smoking and drinking, not a candidate for a freak-show TV shocker. Nor does she belong among the many mothers destined to live on benefits for ever because they are ill, clinically depressed, addicted, sometimes psychotic, the mothers with learning difficulties or caring for severely disabled children. In age, outlook and life story, she is an average single mother with an average tale to tell. The question for us is whether she and her children deserve to be poor in a country so rich.

She doesn't work, like most single mothers with pre-school children, but she will soon join the 57% of single parents who do. Like over half of them, she was married when she had her children. She is thirty-two, just a bit younger than the average age for single parents, which is thirty-six: despite popular imagery, only 2% of single mothers are teenagers. She receives no maintenance from her ex-husband – like two thirds of single mothers. All this explains why her three children, like half the children of single mothers, are growing up in poverty.

Alison comes from a large family, originally from Scotland, who for several generations settled in the West Midlands serving what used to be the region's manufacturing economy. The family remember Alison's grandmother working in the Lucas car-parts factory. Her struggle is part of their identity. After leaving a drunken husband, she brought up seven children on her own. Some of the Murrays have done well: one of Alison's uncles is a minister of religion, one cousin a financial adviser, another a policeman. Some of the clan have a bit of money, some none. Alison's mother did three cleaning jobs simultaneously when they were growing up, but recently she's been promoted to a supervisor's post at BT. Her father earns less, labouring for a temp agency, working at present as a warehouse porter on the minimum wage. One of Alison's brothers still lives at home with her parents and another is married with four children living nearby and doing OK. Aunts, uncles and cousins are scattered around Birmingham.

Alison's great mistake was to fall in love at the age of eighteen with a man of twenty-eight and get pregnant. 'I was daft, no idea about anything. I never tried at school, I was a bit wild and anyway I loved him. All I wanted then was children, babies, that's all I thought about. I look back now and I don't recognize the person I was then. I'd be good at going into schools and warning girls against doing what I did. I'd be good contraception,' she says ruefully.

Her parents wept. They didn't like Dave. But, as all parents must, they forgave their daughter: they themselves had their first child when they were seventeen. Alison and Dave married and moved in with her parents, going onto the council's waiting list. When their second son was born, they moved to a house of their own in Kingstanding. Dave worked in his father's roofing business, and was taking home £500 a week. The couple had a car, a van, a computer with internet access and Sky TV. They also had a third son: Alison's children now range in age from four to thirteen.

It wasn't a happy marriage. Dave was fiercely controlling,

wouldn't let Alison take a job or go out, told her to stay at home while he spent every evening in the pub, drinking more and often hitting her. To her family's despair, she stayed with him – for the children's sake, she thought, and because he still held a powerful sway over her. In some ways he had stopped her ever growing up, keeping her a dependent eighteen-year-old.

How much is she to blame for such folly? Violence is an all too common reason why so many women end up bringing their children up alone. The British Crime Survey reports 12.9 million domestic violence cases a year, and a Council of Europe study (2002) found between 6% and 10% of women in the UK are victims each year. Why do they put up with it? It isn't class specific; violence happens up and down the social range. The difference between Alison and someone in a higher class is the financial consequences of leaving her husband. Eventually, though, it was lack of money not violence which brought Alison's marriage to an end.

Dave's father contracted cancer and the business collapsed, leaving Dave without work. On the dole, it was he who collected most of the family benefits and every week he took the cash to the pub and drank it. 'He was spending the money that was supposed to keep the five of us. I just had the child benefit for us to live on.' She borrowed from the bank to get by and is in retrospect amazed that banks lend to people on benefits. The last straw was when she found out Dave had run up huge debts in their joint names. She threw him out when the electricity was almost cut off with £1,000 outstanding on the bill.

So although she struggles now, paying off debts and trying to feed the children, things are better than they were. Studies show that mothers spend family money better.[6] The lesson here for government policy is obvious: things are worse for families when the father doesn't hand over money. Mothers manage scarce finances better on their own when they draw and control all the money themselves.

When politicians alight on marriage as the solution to the problem of single parenthood, they rarely paint a full picture. Poverty is closely implicated in divorce and the poor are far more likely to divorce. Ask seasoned Citizens Advice Bureau workers or Jobcentre Plus advisers and they confirm the story. A good man earning a wage is an asset, but a bad earner or a high spender precipitates a struggling family into the most abject poverty of all, unseen in the statistics that measure the income of the whole household. Marriage is not necessarily a cure and life is untidy. Human beings make bad decisions all the time and they fall in love with the wrong people. In almost every family of every social class there are stories like Alison's, but the difference is in the financial consequences. Among the middle classes a bad move rarely leads to penury but in the working class the same mistakes make Alison and her children social outcasts as a matter of public policy. Citizens may forgive when confronted with the same conduct in their own clan, but taxpayers don't do mercy.

Poverty relief today, in the form of the social security system, shares traits with relief systems of the last few centuries. The 1832 Poor Law laid the blame for low income squarely on the victim. The needy of working age were given no help: they were told to work, even if there was none. Overseers built punitive workhouses at exorbitant cost, but then found most inmates were frail old people and mothers with babies unable to work. They were still treated harshly, to deter others. These days adults without children on income support are treated the same, deliberately allowed to get poorer every year as their benefits are held down. A decade after Labour took office a single unemployed person received £59 a week, after housing costs, which the Institute for Fiscal Studies calculates as a cut of 8% over ten years in real terms.

A primary cause of child poverty is not lack of marriage but low pay. Over half of families in poverty are in work: paid the minimum wage, what they earn does not lift the household out of poverty. The minimum wage, £5.73 an hour from October 2008, is not a living wage. Even drawing tax credits for the children, the family still often falls under the poverty line, so a family cannot rely on a single breadwinner and the mother must work too, however young her child, if they are to cross that threshold. These days it takes one and a half salaries to get there, and there is still not enough affordable childcare to make the transit possible for many poorer parents.[7]

Some 54% of poor children have a parent in work. Reports, research and reviews repeat this truism but the belief that poverty comes from idleness is deeply entrenched and the benefit scrounger is a prevalent stereotype. It's worth repeating: hard-working people form the bulk of families living below the poverty line. They work in jobs that stitch the fabric of society, cleaning, portering, catering, clerking and caring; they keep us safe and clean, check us out and carry our goods and chattels to and fro. A standard thirty-nine-hour week on the 2007–8 minimum wage would bring in £215.28. That's only 64% of the official poverty line for a family with two children, which is £332 a week. Introduced in 2003, child tax credits, Labour's key tool in reducing poverty, do top up income from work more generously than ever before. 'Making work pay' was the slogan, and tax credits ensure that people are almost always better off in work than relying on benefits; but they do not guarantee an end to poverty.

Low-paying employers benefit greatly from Labour's introduction of tax credits. The credits amount to a back-hander from the taxpayer – not something that employers' organizations ever acknowledge or give thanks for. Employers should imagine what would happen if these credits were suddenly withdrawn. All these people would have to drop out of work and fall back on benefits until pay rates rose to a level above benefits. It would demonstrate just how much the taxpayer subsidizes low-paying companies.

Could the minimum wage be raised? Economists draw supply and demand curves; in theory if you raise the price of supply then demand will fall and jobs will be lost. The trouble is, they have no idea where the curves intersect. When the minimum wage was introduced in 1998 the Tories and the CBI preached doom and gloom, predicting a million jobs would be lost once employers were stopped from paying £1.50 an hour. In the subsequent decade during which the minimum has risen, some 3 million jobs were created and successive annual reports from the Low Pay Commission found no deleterious effects. At some notional point demand for labour would fall because the minimum wage had risen too high – but so far the public house in

Newcastle, care home in Hampshire and supermarket in Bristol have not hit it, and each would probably have different tolerances for higher pay. Open-minded economists say suck it and see: keep pushing up the rate until it starts causing job losses. Some suggest more regional or sectoral variation in the minimum, though a national rate is simpler to police. Higher rates eventually mean more costly services and the public would have to consent to shifting the trade-off between fairness and cheap services; but if the person washing the dishes can't get by on their pay, then we aren't paying enough for the restaurant meal, and it's time we did.

The wonder is not that some people skive on benefits, but that so many go to work to earn barely more than benefits. Compare governments' efforts to prevent scrounging with the phenomenal pull of the work ethic. The urge that drives parents in a poor household to work at menial jobs without the prospect of promotion for not much more than they would get if they stayed at home comes from their deep reservoirs of pride, self-respect, a desire to be useful and their impulse to inhabit mainstream life.

After the low paid, the next largest group of poor people are single parents, or at least the 46% of them who are not working. Here is terra firma for entrenched attitudes: single parents don't raise the tricky questions of merit and distribution of rewards. It is plainly their fault. An army of social scientists, researchers and politicians have sought to stop women having children and (failing hopelessly) to make fathers pay. What makes girls get pregnant too young, they ask, wringing their hands – though the number of teenage mothers is low and falling. As a proportion of all mothers, the number of single mothers is static, not rising. Latter-day Victorians warn that welfare risks creating a permanent stock of them. Under the influence of American think-tanks Tory policy makers keep reaching for crudely behaviourist models, in which taking and giving sums of money will keep relationships going. But the evidence shows that financial (dis)incentives don't work. A mother's income falls when she separates from a partner, and remains at 12% below pre-separation levels over subsequent years. Which does not stop the sundering.[8]

The rest of us, moneyed and/or lucky, may gamble, drink, choose a disastrous partner, fall into debt, behave badly or get pregnant unintentionally (most women do at some time). Friends forgive our faults, sympathize and accept that most people blunder sometimes. The mistakes of the poor make them society's problem, and the way they are then targeted for moral obloquy is one of the greatest inequalities of all. Remember what Hamlet said: 'use every man after his desert, and who should 'scape whipping?'.

Alison Murray may be a lone parent but she is a good mother, bright and energetic. Her children are none the less at risk, for all kinds of reasons. They are upset by their father's violence and departure, scared by the sudden downward crash in the family's fortunes and anxious about their mother's debts and money problems. Still, the two eldest are full of plans: one to be a PE teacher, the other to be a literacy teacher – he likes his literacy classes in primary school. Maybe they'll make it; their mother will certainly help them all she can. But maybe life on the estate will drag them down. They are good boys now, but how far will Alison be able to protect them from bad company in their teens?

In affluent societies, going without in childhood appears to be driving more and more teenagers into gangs whose watchwords are 'get rich or die trying'. If you've never had a birthday party or a brand new present, it's hard to Just Say No to wads of drug-courier money. Children aren't stupid and they instinctively calculate the odds. Take the criminal path and the middle-class child jeopardizes a certain destiny ahead – university, a well-paid job, a nice house, the good life. On the estate a child doing badly jeopardizes only a remote chance of a job that pays. Deferring will not lead to much gratification later, so why not take a slice now? Alison will be just one of thousands of mothers in the area trying to keep her teenagers from danger, and the odds are stacked against her.

Alison's plight, like that of many families on income support for a time, is deepened by debt. She is paying off a loan from the Social Fund at a rate of £12.50 a week. This is a cash-limited pot of money from which social security officials can, at their discretion, make payments to cover emergencies or to buy necessary furniture and equipment. She owes £10 a week for the old electricity debt. There's £10 a week outstanding on a credit card bill that was run up to pay for the car from better times that sits outside. It has no MOT, no money to run it and is not worth anything now. The internet and Sky went long ago.

The man responsible for these debts pays nothing. The family see him in and out of local pubs but he never visits the children, which has left them angry and upset. He has found work with a cousin and he gloated to Alison not long ago that he was expecting a £7,000 tax rebate, so he must be earning quite a bit, she reckons, although none of it will come her way. The Child Support Agency (CSA) has failed her and she's given up even thinking about money from him. He says he has no obligation to pay because it was she who threw him out; he has another girlfriend now. The CSA has been a disaster since its creation by the Conservatives in 1993 – though the system it replaced was no better at making absent fathers pay for their children. It was devised to save the social security system money, with no incentive for mothers on benefit to cooperate since they got nothing but the aggravation of angry fathers resisting the CSA's demands. As one attempted reform followed another, it was not so much computers or filing systems that brought the system to a grinding halt as the fathers' deliberate obstruction. The result is that only 52% of single mothers who are eligible for maintenance have an agreement or an order for the absent father to pay. In only 62% of the cases where the CSA has issued a maintenance order has the father actually paid. In 2007 some £3.5 billion was owed to mothers.

Dave is all too typical and no wonder Alison, like many mothers, has given up trying, despite recent new rules that would allow her to keep more of the money Dave should have been paying her. Estranged partners with children (like Alison) living on income support were allowed to keep a portion of the money they received in maintenance before they sacrificed benefit payments; that amount is being raised this year to £20 per week. Yet Alison, rid of him, has surprised herself, finding herself more resilient than she ever realized. She is hopeful, lively and determined to find her way. And there is help. 'Maxine is a wonder,' she says of her personal adviser in the local branch of the Department of Work and Pensions' Jobcentre Plus. 'She is always there for me, and she's getting me back on my feet.' Alison has new ambitions and for the first time in years she is optimistic.

'There are bad days, very bad days,' she says. 'Yesterday I cried, I had a real good blub, which I haven't done for ages. What got to me was my mother's kindness and I cried walking all the way home from hers in the dark last night. I didn't want the kids to see.' She rubs her eyes at the memory. 'My mum called to say she's been down to the shops and got a whole bag of food for me, things that were on "special". She always says that, when I know they weren't specials at all. I walked up to hers and came back with a bag of bread, cakes, sausages, fruit, broccoli, pasta, the lot. What would I do without my mum? My brother too, he comes round with cans of soup and stuff for me.' She sniffs.

'Before you came to see me, I went round to my friends, three of them living like me on income support. I asked how they managed, because you were interested. All of them said the same. They didn't, they couldn't get by on their own. The only thing that kept them going was good families helping out. I don't know how anyone with kids gets by if they haven't got a good family – and mine's just the best there is.'

But they still do without. 'It's things for the children I mind most. I mean I never have new clothes, all charity shop for me and them, but I don't mind that much. It's the things you can't do for them.' She lists activities most families take for granted, things she can never afford. They never go swimming. They never go to the cinema. They never take a train. They never have a day's holiday and a trip by bus to the park for a picnic is the best they can manage. 'Last time the gardeners there let the kids help with the planting, so we're going back soon to see how our plants are doing.' She has been in touch with One Parent Families/Gingerbread, the self-help group which organizes cheap holidays by coach to stay in caravans by the sea, but they can't even afford that for all four of them. 'Even if I could, we'd have no spending money at all. How can you go to the seaside and spend nothing at all for a week?'

Christmas and birthdays are worst. In a charity shop she found a second-hand out-of-date PlayStation for Jamie, her oldest boy, with some second-hand games. 'He was pleased, and he didn't say anything about it being old. But I knew most of his friends had up-to-date ones, Xbox and games he doesn't even know, so he can't join in their conversations.' Jamie is an aware boy and never asks for things, no designer T-shirts or branded trainers or outings his friends go on all the time. If he is asked to write an essay about his holidays he says he makes an answer up. But at thirteen his feet are size 9 and strong school shoes cost £40. He gets free school meals but the £1.60 allowance buys him much less in the school canteen than his friends have: they have much more to spend, buying Coke and crisps and sweets. There is all the difference in the world between choosing not to have Coke and crisps, and being too poor to buy them ever. Jamie talks about how he used to go to Aston Villa matches with his dad, but they can't afford that any more. 'We did go once on a special day for families when there were empty seats, because Charlton never brings many supporters, but even then it cost us £20.' Then there are the birthday parties. They often don't go when asked because they can't afford a nice enough present to take. They certainly never give a birthday party themselves. How would they afford luxury food, let alone going-home bags?

Alison's family is warm and well-enough housed and they don't lack for food. Compared to when her grandmother was young raising seven children alone, Alison's standard of living looks like one of untold luxury and comfort. By coincidence, Polly Toynbee too worked briefly in the Lucas plant in Birmingham, researching a book on work in the early 1970s at the same time that Alison's grandmother would have been there. It was strongly unionized and the pay wasn't bad by the standard of the times. But those pre-war houses were cold – just one coal fire in the front room and lino on the floor with a small rug, no carpet. The butcher's shop near the factory gates sold tripe and offal which few families eat now. Most people at Lucas's didn't have a holiday away from home, usually just an occasional day out. Most had no telephone, some had no fridge, some no television and virtually none could afford the cars they were helping to manufacture.

But that was then, and it's what you have relative to those around you. Living standards have improved by a third in the last decade and will probably rise by roughly the same again in the next ten years. As the basic minimum moves up, the country gets richer and everyone can afford more – but what matters is where you stand, your position in the pecking order. Put yourself in the position of a child and remember how the very stuff of childhood, especially at school, is comparison. Talk to any primary-school teacher about the first days at school for a child from a household at or below the poverty line. It doesn't take long in the playground to sort out where they stand in relation to the rest. School uniforms help conceal the inability to pay, so long as the clothing is sensible and cheap. Even where schools try hard to minimize class differences, money always talks. The children who are perfectly turned out, with the most desirable branded lunch boxes and trainers, showing off the newest toys, displaying the social and educational skills that come from maybe three years in a nursery, will instinctively draw together, sharing interests, words, ideas and experiences. With every subsequent year spent in school, social background tells more strongly. Maintaining your self-esteem and your enthusiasm for school when you are at the bottom of that pecking order requires exceptional strength of character, talent or good fortune. Although the quality of parenting makes a difference, poverty for the most part is destiny.

Alison will try. She is quite a role model for her children. She has been going part-time to the local further education college and has passed seven GCSEs. Because she's on income support, she can put her youngest boy into the Busy Bees crèche at the college for free – otherwise studying would have been impossible. She has nearly completed a business administration course and when her youngest starts primary school, she plans to do a year's full-time beautician's course. 'That's what I want to be and with all my qualifications, I know there is a lot of work. I'll have no trouble finding the job I want.' She says she has always wanted to work, but her husband wouldn't let her. 'I think it's completely wrong for mothers to sit at home on income support once their kids are in full-time school. I wouldn't think of it. I'm going out to work, for good, and I'm going to do well. Watch me and see!'

Where did all this get-up-and-go come from, in this woman who describes how downtrodden she used to be? She says the New Deal for Lone Parents has been the saving of her. 'Maxine has stood by me for a few years now, telling me what I can do, helping me find the childcare, telling me things I didn't know. I didn't know that I can get a job grant of money to go for an interview, so I can have respectable clothes. I was thinking I could never go for a job in my old charity-shop stuff. Maxine took me to the college the first time. She is always there, and I drop in and see her a lot.' Here is a long-term investment by the state in Alison that looks likely to pay off.

Labour swept to power in 1997 with ready-made plans for a New Deal for all categories of the unemployed to help get them back to work, paid for by a £5 billion windfall tax on the profitable utilities that had been privatized by the Tories. It was popular, successful and greeted with enthusiasm by most of those it was designed to help, shifting many of the long-term unemployed back to work. The New Deal for Lone Parents, devised soon after Labour came to power, required them to attend a regular interview at their local Jobcentre Plus and hear what opportunities are available. They are under no obligation to work until their youngest child is sixteen. In October 2008 that becomes twelve and drops to seven in 2010. The number of single parents who work has risen in the years of the New Deal from 46% to 56%. The 2010 target is 70%.

At the interviews advisers calculate how much better off

mothers would be by working: their credits, costs and benefits. It can be a finely balanced judgement, especially with a child under school age. Good childcare can be hard to find and parents have to pay 20% of the cost, although many end up paying much more. For some women, taking a job may mean earning paltry extra sums while leaving a child with a minder or nursery they are not happy with.

Labour knew that expanding good-quality childcare was essential to get mothers back to work, but there is still too little investment to ensure every child is looked after by fully trained carers and nursery teachers. Labour ministers used to visit Scandinavia and return determined to copy its nursery system but, back in this far lower-tax country, they tried to do it on a shoestring. In Sweden every child can have a place in a neighbourhood nursery from the age of one, and half the staff are graduates who have studied child development, psychology, care and education. In the UK many children, especially those in private nurseries, are cared for by young girls, underpaid and under-trained, who themselves failed at school. The children may be cuddled and safely supervised, but it's precisely the poorest children who need the most stimulation. It is they who would benefit most from the intellectual stimulus of well-educated and trained nursery carers, compensating for all they are not getting at home.

Kingstanding portrays the ordinary, unspectacular face of poverty today. The paths that individuals take are not determined by statistics and things may well improve for Alison, whose optimism is infectious. But working as a beautician is unlikely ever to pay enough to lift the Murrays' household income up to the median, let alone the average. What becomes of Alison's children, growing up in poverty? Will they remain part of a cycle of deprivation, trapped within a culture with little chance of escape to the bright, sunny uplands of the better off? Individual opportunities of course vary. Some make it, others stumble. But it doesn't take much to tip a family downwards when they live too close to the edge.

CHAPTER 5

Emily and Callum

The number 35 bus was trundling towards Clapham Junction on a grey early afternoon, that desultory time of day when pensioners and mothers with young children are the only people at a loose end. Two pushchairs were parked in the pram slot. One was empty but in the other a shaven-headed little boy of about two was writhing about, giving intermittent shrieks, like a lorry starting to reverse. And reverse was what he wanted, strapped into a pram jammed right against the wall, so he couldn't either see out of the window or what was going on inside the bus. He kicked hard to push the pram backwards, clutching in one hand a half-empty packet of Monster Munch, some of which fell on the floor as he struggled to get out.

His mother was sitting on the seat beside the pram, gazing out of the window. She was perhaps twenty, her hair scraped back in a punishing ponytail, gold-hooped rings in her ears, a tight pink jacket and jeans. Her jaw was set and she didn't look at her son, as if she would rather not be associated with this shouting, wriggling thing. When another spray of Monster Munch scattered on the floor she grabbed the packet from his hand and cuffed him round his bristly little head, not hard, but enough to set him yelling full pelt, his mouth wide open and dribbling out half-chewed crisps. Everyone else in the bus looked the other way.

'Shut up, Callum! Shut up, shut up will you.' He screamed the more. 'We'll get out at the next stop.' No let-up. 'I won't take you to the fucking park if you don't fucking shut it!' The boy stopped, maybe because of the threats or perhaps he had just run out of steam. 'I don't want to take you to the bleeding park, do I? I hate the park!' By now her performance seemed to be addressed to everyone in the bus, although no one was looking her way. 'I do everything for you, and all you do is show me up!' Callum was now quiet, sullen and angry-looking. He had retreated into some realm of his own, no longer kicking at the bus wall.

Maybe it was just a bad day for Callum. Maybe his mother was in an off mood – afternoons alone with a young child get to most mothers. But it's a fair guess that most people on the bus were thinking the same. Poor kid, what chance has he got? Why doesn't she pick him up out of the pram, tuck him onto her lap, let him look out of the window and chat to him instead of shouting? Maybe onlookers took another sideways look at her and wondered what kind of life she had with what kind of mother or grandmother. Did she get enough kindness or warmth in her own childhood to pass on to her own son? She had a stony look that made it easy to imagine her mother had never cuddled and played with her, talked, laughed, listened or taken pleasure and pride in her.

This is just a tableau, an episode. It's a vignette on a life lived in frustration and disappointment, hopes weighed down, a life lived by people whose experiences through the generations taught them to expect little. That seemed to be the message Callum was learning. No windows.

The other pushchair was empty because the little girl it belonged to had been taken out and was sitting on her mother's knee at the front of the bus. They were playing finger games – 'round and round the garden and tickling under there'. They were talking about what was happening out of the window – a schoolboy football match on the common, big dogs, little dogs, fat crows pecking at an overflowing litter bin.

The mother took out a book shaped like a bus, and before she could start reading the little girl sang loudly and out of tune, 'Wheels on the bus go round and round,' and an elderly woman behind her smiled. 'Emily on the bus,' she shouted, catching the woman's eye and talking to her over her mother's shoulder. 'Emily on the bus! Mummy on the bus!' The woman responded with pleasure: 'Now Emily, that's a nice name. And you sing nicely too.' Emily chuckled, then suddenly shy she buried her head in her mother's coat. 'I hope she's not bothering you?' her mother said quietly, in that precise, intelligently modulated tone, not especially posh but suggesting education, maybe even generations of well-brought-up lives. They chatted politely for a few minutes, Emily listening intently until it was time to get back in her pram.

The Camel Train: The stragglers behind

At Clapham Junction, the two pushchairs bumped down the step onto the pavement together and headed in opposite directions. Almost certainly for life. It doesn't take much imagination or much knowledge of British society to guess the likely fate of Callum and Emily. Maybe they will meet up on their first day in primary school aged five, Emily bubbling with words and stories, books and songs, already writing her name and recognizing letters. She makes friends easily because she's a talker and she's used to playing all kinds of games, sitting and listening, joining in, sharing, taking turns. She expects adults to like her and talk to her. She expects her first term at school to be full of fun and excitement, taking her projects home to proud parents as fascinated as she is by every little thing she says and does.

On his first day Callum may be at sea. He expects quite rough and surly treatment from adults, and maybe he treats other children roughly and gets into trouble for it. Words are not his principal means of communication; he has never been talked to much, and has been listened to even less. Sitting still and attending to words is difficult. They float in the air just out of reach of his untrained concentration. Dashing about is the only fun he knows. Life courses are set long before school starts and social research confirms what onlookers on the bus instinctively assumed. Class is destiny.

Lack of money, structural unfairness and family circumstances do not determine life's outcomes. Sociology predicts trends, not each individual's fate. Maybe Emily won't grow up to do law, medicine or teacher training at university. Maybe she will take a dark swerve and end in the gutter with a needle in her arm. Maybe she will suffer a shocking depressive illness that sends her juddering down another course, but it would take something extreme to unseat her. From that first bright day in infant school she will go on to receive a good education she will make good use of, leading to a well-paid job and marriage or partnership with someone from her own social milieu, with her background and income. We can even put a figure on her security. Emily is fifteen times more likely to stay in the middle class when she grows up than Callum is to move up into the middle class.[1] She will almost certainly stay where she is, socially speaking, and so will he.

Callum might escape. If he goes to a brilliant nursery or Sure Start he might arrive at primary school keen and able to learn. A perceptive primary or secondary teacher might encourage his progress, or maybe he is an exceptional boy, endowed with some characteristic or talent allowing him to defy the gravity of his background. Football? Music? Maths? Or just a burning ambition to succeed? But his upbringing stacks the odds heavily against him.

Alison Murray's children have a gentle and protective mother from a large and affectionate family who will all try to do their best for them. It's easy to see what can be done to help them all on their way. More money would make all the difference to the Murrays' quality of life – and Alison's New Deal adviser was already transforming her future trajectory, showing what state help of the right kind at the right time can do. But there are other children considerably worse off, where generations of hardship or cruelty of one kind or another have taken their toll, passed on from parent to child. They are that 2% the government worries over most. Of course we know nothing about the real Callum, but let him stand as an imaginary symbol for all those children in families that need a great deal more help from the start, the ones described as 'hard to reach'.

Following a sample of children born in 1970 into their adulthood, Leon Feinstein of the London Institute of Education monitored the progress of bright children from lower socio-economic backgrounds against less bright children from high socio-economic backgrounds. At twenty-two months you might have a very bright Callum, naturally endowed with a capacity to learn. Imagine he is objectively far more able than Emily, who might be naturally slow, despite her background. But within a short time Feinstein found the natural advantages of bright but poor children eroding. At the age of six their scores are the same. From then on their paths cross over and the less talented Emilys rise while the much brighter Callums sink. His early advantage is lost for ever by the age of ten.[2] Nurture beats nature.

Consider one of the great nostrums of business, much repeated by New Labour in recent times. They say you can't push up the taxes to help children like Callum without harming the economy. Yet Callum and all the failing children like him, the ones kept down, the ones who never get a sniff of possibility, represent waste on a huge scale. Research for the End Child Poverty campaign, which includes all the big children's charities and ninety other organizations, estimated that child poverty costs the country £40 billion a year in direct costs and lost productivity, which amounts to £12 a week for every citizen. Given a chance, these are children who as adults might innovate, create new businesses, prove steady employees, contribute to the buying and selling that makes the economy spin. They would no longer cost large sums in social security, in mental illness, in crime and punishment or in all the other expenses of failure. If more and better focused public spending can save Callum then the case for raising the tax to support him is irrefutable.

There is no simple formula and it is an uphill task to intervene in ways that make an important difference. First we have to understand why background is so powerful. American researchers Betty Hart and Todd Risley have shown the vital importance of language at the youngest age.[3] The fate of children, their future education and social class lies in the words they use and the way they are encouraged to speak when they are very young. Words are everything, the basic tool for thought, argument, reasoning and making sense of a confusing world. In the first three years of life, especially in the first two years, the developing brain absorbs language and all the concepts, emotions and cultural richness it embodies. To listen, talk and be listened to is everything to a young child.

Hart and Risley led a team that recorded children in their first years. The project allocated them to three broad groups – families on welfare (receiving social security benefits), working-class families and professional families. Painstakingly, the researchers counted all the words children would hear and speak as they interacted with parents or care-givers, analysing hours and hours of recordings. What emerged from this epic was just how stark are the differences between the three groups' early experiences.

The results can be expressed in hard numbers. By the age of four the child from a professional family will have had 50 million words addressed to it. A working-class child will have heard 30 million, but the children from families on welfare will hear 12 million. Here was another shocking fact: by the age of three the child of the professional family will have a bigger vocabulary than the adult parents of the welfare child.

The team looked at not just the number and variety of words but also at the ways in which children are spoken to. Remember Callum's mum on the bus: the team asked whether children were listened to and given choices. Did their parents explain the things happening around them and in what tone of voice? By the age of three the professional child has had 700,000 encouragements addressed to it, with 80,000 discouragements. Compare that with the welfare child who will have had 60,000 encouragements – more than ten times fewer – and twice as many discouragements. The working-class child falls between the two. These are the numbers behind the different chances in life for Callum and Emily. Love, praise, reason and explanation in millions of words grow the brain and open up the mind. The potential of the child without those most precious things withers.

Children in this study were measured again between the ages of nine and ten. Hart and Risley were 'awestruck at how well our measures of accomplishments at three, predicted language skill at nine to ten'. The years of schooling between had added little value after the age of three: it was already too late. Their study put flesh on old bones. Here is a social truth we have known for a long time. What matters most is what happens very young. We also know what works in mitigating the disadvantages of being born into poor families. We must change priorities within education, to redirect money to the most effective early-years programmes.

Labour gave three- and four-year-olds fifteen hours of free nursery teaching a week, and inaugurated a national programme in which, eventually, every child can find an affordable place. Since parents have to pay, and too few places are free for needy children, more needs to be spent. The 'hard to reach' families that could make most use of these opportunities may be netted by the specialists now being appointed to seek them out. The expansion of nursery education in recent years is a great step forward, and reports from the Office for Standards in Education (Ofsted) say what is on offer does well enough for most children. But Callum's life course will only be changed by more intensive programmes. The Effective Provision of Pre-School Education project shows that high-quality nursery teaching makes all the difference. Early intervention needs to be followed by school programmes aimed at children at risk of failing. But all this is intensive and expensive. Will future governments have the patience to keep investing, although results may not show for twenty years or more, when the children have grown up?

Society, including the very affluent behind their gates, can never escape Callum. He becomes, all too easily, 'a problem'. He turns into an anti-social hoody who – the papers rage – has to be castigated and even imprisoned, at vast expense. When he gets out he'll come along and, in Ian Dury's crisp words, piss in your swimming pool. He haunts the nightmares of the well off. Everyone's well-being improves in a society where everyone enjoys as decent a life as is humanly possible.

The Camel Train: The stragglers behind

Children can be helped most at their very youngest, but we spend least on those children most at risk of not hearing and using the words on which their future capacity depends. Nursery education for the under-fives gets least per head, yet this is where every pound spent is likely to do most to stop children falling behind. Once children get to primary school, it's already too late for many. The evidence from Norway, Sweden and Denmark is strong. Gosta Esping-Andersen concludes that 'high quality and universal child care is, in tandem with low child poverty, a likely factor behind Scandinavia's success in reducing social inheritance. Incontrovertible proof is difficult to furnish, but all the data point in this direction. Most importantly, the decline in social inheritance effects on educational attainment coincides almost perfectly with the period (1970s–80s) in which child care attendance became the norm.'[4]

No one is saying we should spend less on primary and secondary schools, but tough value-for-money assessments need to be made throughout the education system, focusing on where programmes do most to attenuate the intergenerational lock on Callum. Thanks to her mother and father, Emily would thrive almost anywhere. Money and the attention of policy makers have to be channelled to where Callum might benefit most, and that is in the earliest years of his life.

CHAPTER 6

Aim higher

It's a straight line from Brent to Oxford along the A40 and M40, no great distance, an hour or so by car from north-west London. Yet this excursion by pupils from Brent's Capital City Academy to the university spires crosses the deepest ravines of the UK's social divide. The yellow limestone buildings of St John's College left the Brent pupils almost breathless with amazement. They had seen nothing like it and it was nothing like they imagined a university to be. Nor were those arches and fan vaults much like the universities and further education colleges most of them are likely to attend.

The pupils of Capital City Academy have been sent to Oxford to urge them to aspire, and over one weekend are given a tantalizing taste of life behind the college gates among those manicured lawns. The AimHigher programme had chosen the likeliest sixteen-year-olds in their GCSE year from this Brent school to spend two days in Oxford. They were staying in rooms in St John's of such comfort and spaciousness they found it hard to believe they could be for their use. They were briefly sampling a world of privilege most of them barely knew existed.

Some 72% of Brent school students are from ethnic minorities – and virtually all these sixteen-year-olds were black or brown. Race is only another ingredient in the story of social injustice and social distance. That black children are disproportionately poor is a cultural disaster, but once poor, it is generally their poverty that holds them back. Nearly a third of the school's intake live in bad housing, below the government's decency standard. AimHigher starts by targeting year 9–11 pupils with homework clubs, summer schools, revision classes, taster courses and mentoring. These university visits for older pupils are designed to persuade them to strive for A-level and university success.

Virtually none of their parents had any further education and many had only ever been outside their thin slice of London once before, on a school trip to the Isle of Wight. So it was hardly surprising that their idea of higher education was vague. None of the group had seen a university before, though one girl mentioned a local Brent college she had walked past. What had they imagined university to be? They said 'like a prison', 'really hard work, and no social life', 'horrible, worse than school and locked in all the time'. It is comforting to imagine that every child these days has the same basic opportunities: even in the most deprived areas schools help a few ambitious and determined children plant their feet on the ladder upwards. The trouble is, people say complacently, families just don't try hard enough and they lack the ambition to push their children out of their own social milieu. Parents who failed at school may even encourage their children to be like them, saying 'our family was never any good at school' or 'we're not the clever sort'.

Unlike the children of graduates, the Brent students had no one to tell them tales of student life, no sister or cousin to whisper to them that university for most young people is a time of lounging around and enjoyment, interspersed with panicky bursts of academic work; no one to share the anxieties of upwards social mobility and sometimes the deep sense of loss, captured recently in Hanif Kureishi's novel *Something to Tell You* (2008) or, a generation back, Raymond Williams's *Border Country* (1960). In a profoundly unequal society, moving up a social class can feel as alienating as moving to Australia. Some parents don't want to let their children go, and some children don't wish to emigrate out of their family circumstance. When that social distance is so wide, of course it is much harder for young people to cross it. It's not surprising that the countries that are most equal, with the least distance from top to bottom, tend to be the societies where it is easiest for the cleaner's child to take a top university place.

Undergraduates had volunteered to show them round, to talk about life and work at Oxford. It was the bedrooms that astonished and pleased them most about their trip. At home the Brent pupils shared rooms with siblings but here was a room of their own, with their own bathroom, use of a kitchen and common room. They asked simple questions: were students ever allowed beyond those great college walls? Yes, all day and all night.

They asked if they could have visitors and if their parents could come and see them? Yes, any time and even have a cheap room to stay in overnight. And was term time just twenty-four weeks of the year? Yes, but they could stay on in the holidays if they liked. They could even have people to stay in their room too, if they signed them in. The opposite sex? Yes! Wow! 'Oh no you don't!' said their teacher smartly, for fear they would start experimenting with student life straight away.

One of their undergraduate guides had just put on a Terry Pratchett play in the small theatre in St John's. The Brent kids were told they could put on any play they liked in one of Oxford's many theatres, which astounded them. Where could they do their washing? Use of washing machines in the college was £1 a time, which one of the girls thought a bit steep. There was every sport available they could imagine and every club and activity under the Oxford spires.

How many wanted to come here? Well over half of the teenagers raised their hands eagerly, some punching the air with excitement. Then talk turned to work as they were told they would need three As at A-level. 'We can do that!' was the response from many. Oxford only considers three hard academic subjects. These undergraduate guides all had maths, further maths, physics and chemistry, though one had done French for fun. All of them were medical, IT or engineering students and most had four As, though officially the university never asked for more than three.

'Not PE, not drama A-level?' asked one Brent boy, who planned to take both these at a sixth-form college. Not general studies either, and probably not sociology or psychology they were told, which left many of the Brent pupils crestfallen. Their kindly mentors offered a dose of realism. 'It is hard work. Although we are very free, we have to work hard too. But you can work when you like.' They didn't want to dampen the Brent pupils' enthusiasm but they felt they should warn them. 'I'm afraid no subject here is a doss.' What about English, a girl asked, hoping to have found something less relentlessly tough. The young university admissions tutor hosting this event shook her head. 'English is no doss either. You have to do an author a week from the year 1100 to the present day. That means you have to read a book a day, at least seven books a week. It means working seven hours a day.' One or two of the most intense and studious Brent pupils nodded that they could do it: they were already studying hard to get near the three As at A-level stand-ard. But others gasped at such hard work, and shook their heads solemnly.

Privately, Peter Boursnell, a deputy head who coordinated AimHigher for all Brent schools, was not overly optimistic that many or perhaps any of these pupils would make it. Their teacher, though, would have no defeatism. 'You can do it!' she said to them over and over again. Christalina was their head of year, a remarkable young black woman, elegant, witty and plainly admired by her pupils. She had that rare teacherly gift, giving them passionate loyalty, concern and a measure of inti-macy, yet a firmness that ensured their respect.

Did the Brent students know that over half the students at Oxford and Cambridge come from private schools? They had no idea and it shocked them. Privately educated pupils would be getting a lot of special teaching in small classes to train them for

Oxbridge, but their teacher remained positive. 'If you were at an interview, what could you say you all have that children from private schools don't have?' That stumped them for a moment. 'We're streetwise?' asked one doubtfully, pulling his woolly hat down over his large ears. As they struggled to find her meaning they gazed at the St John's undergraduates, so different from themselves. Yet only one of the student guides had been privately educated, at Ampleforth, the Catholic boarding school. One was a Muslim from Edinburgh studying medicine. Most were white and came from high-flying state schools in good neighbourhoods that regularly sent pupils to Oxbridge. Already these undergraduates had acquired the academic aura; how sharply their woolly-bearded seriousness, their kindly earnestness and bright whiteness contrasted with the mostly black Brent kids in urban fashions with sharply razored, sculpted and combed hairstyles. Here on display was the great fissure in class, race, style, attitude, background, life-experience and confidence that AimHigher is trying to bridge. 'Come on,' their teacher urged them. 'Think. Well, I can tell you what you should say. Just think what you all have to do to get three As at A-level compared with private-school kids. How many of you have nowhere quiet to work?' Two thirds raised their hands. 'How many of you have only learnt to speak English in the last few years?' Amazingly, nearly half raised their hands. 'How many of you had very little school experience before you came to our school?' About a quarter. 'Do you have people at home to push and help you, people to pay for extra lessons? No! So you will have got your A-levels because of your own efforts in spite of difficulties that those private-school kids never even thought of.'

She urged them on, motivating and encouraging. 'When you get to university you will all have plenty of untapped potential but maybe those pupils crammed to the eyeballs in private schools may never get any better. You will have proved you can work hard in hard circumstances with no spoon-feeding. You know what it is to work despite a lot of distraction and lots of temptations.' She didn't need to spell it out loud, as the AimHigher coordinator murmured that gangs with money and drugs lurk in their neighbourhoods to trip, intimidate and tempt at every turn. Staying on for A-levels was itself a triumph: many had seen older siblings take disastrously wrong turns.

Their teacher's determination cheered the pupils. They left the gleaming spires with a vision of university as a place of pleasure – a new thought and perhaps the most important one at this stage in their lives. Would any of them make it back to Oxford after their A-levels? Their teacher thought two of them were in with a chance as they were exceptionally clever. But it would depend on admissions tutors appreciating how much they had overcome in how short a time. Several were Afghan refugees who in the course of the two days had talked movingly of American gunships firing on their towns and villages. One boy was African-Caribbean, UK-born and in care for years. In year 9 he barely attended school and was shunted from pillar to post, but once settled in year 10 he had become pupil of the year and was now destined to do well, despite everything. Would an Oxbridge tutor ever hear these stories – and get to assess how their potential stacked up against the attainment of a young person who had no obstacles to overcome?

The Brent students will likely find themselves in a rust-stained concrete former polytechnic not far from home in London, to save money. A seductive glimpse of Oxford might leave them feeling they failed, when to make it to university at all would be success against extreme odds. By the end of the visit, sobered, they could see that gaining a place at Oxford would be like climbing Everest without oxygen or crampons. But they came away exhilarated, all of them vowing to try harder, to work hard, to get the best possible marks at GCSE and then at A-level.

If only the tabloids had been there to meet them and listen to their stories. By coincidence the Universities and Colleges Admissions Service had proposed that same week that applicants state their parents' occupations and ethnic backgrounds and whether they had a university-level education. The information would be passed to admissions tutors to help them gauge potential. This modest proposal caused outrage and uproar in the right-wing press. Here was the *Daily Mail*'s leader: 'Forget aspiration, hard work and brilliance. Forget open, healthy competition for those coveted degree courses that so benefit the future wealth of the UK. You may be among the brightest and the best, but if you come from the despised middle classes you're going to be disadvantaged the moment you fill in your application form. Don't for a moment believe this is all in the cause of innocent research. It is as cold-blooded an attempt at social engineering as can be imagined. Labour is rigging the system and dumbing down higher education.'

Fairness is painful. Places at Oxford and Cambridge are positional goods, meaning their supply is inherently limited. Equal opportunity for all would mean more students bidding for them: some who now get the glittering prizes would lose in future. The middle classes, many of them the sons and daughters of those who climbed the social ladder in the 1960s, have been consolidating their hold on high-status jobs and blocking the upward ascent of children from lower-class backgrounds, with the right-wing press as their standard bearers. Ministers avert their eyes from incipient class struggle. Plenty of room on top, they repeat, like the old-fashioned bus conductor, but in reality some may have to come down the stairs before others can rise.

Of course the UK is more classless, by appearance: thanks to Primark, rich and poor look and dress more alike. We pretend the UK is an open society, sharing a myth with Americans that we live in a land of opportunity. Look at the justice minister Jack Straw or the private equity mega-star Damon Buffini, who both made it from single-parent families on grim estates.

But social mobility gets exaggerated. The generation born in the 1940s and 1950s saw an extraordinary post-war change in class destiny. Professional and administrative jobs expanded and today's fifty-somethings remember the trauma and excitement of moving out of their parents' class. They wrongly assume this social progress was an inevitable part of modernity, not a temporary phenomenon.

Instead mobility slowed perceptibly in the 1980s; the data may even show a halt. Surrey University's Jo Blanden and colleagues sampled the origins and destinations among those who were born in 1958 and those born in 1970.[1] The first group reached the age of thirty just as Mrs Thatcher was nearing her apogee; the second were thirty just as Blair and Brown were hitting their stride. The cohort born in 1958, who started work in the 1970s, struck gold; desirable, well-paid jobs were expanding in number just as they entered the labour market. Then the clock turned back. Those born in 1970, setting out to work in the late 1980s and early 1990s, found the door to opportunity shut, and they slid back to where, socially speaking, they began. Many did move on and up: 16% of the sons of the poorest homes born in 1970 reached the top quarter. But 37% stayed put, just as 40% of the sons of the best-off families in 1970s stayed right where they were. Two thirds of the total have not strayed far from their parental class.

Social class of origin has become more important to destination. The earnings of the birth cohort of 1970 were more closely tied to their parents' earnings than those of the 1958 cohort. As wage and income distribution widened from the late 1970s onwards so mobility slowed down, upwards and downwards. If you split people up into four groups according to their income, in a perfectly mobile society a quarter of the children from each group should be distributed equally as adults between all four groups. Sociologists look at people exchanging occupational slots over time, moving down as well as up. In a fluid society the chances of people of different class origins ending up in one class rather than another would be similar – they might go up, they might go down. We hear all the time about competitiveness and open markets but these precepts don't seem to hold for society. We get upset when cartels fix prices, but the middle classes' skill at erecting barriers to social fluidity is similar.

The Brent challenge is not just fighting to raise aspirations but to overwhelm those defending the bastions of privilege their pupils want to enter. Top jobs, like places at Oxford colleges, are strictly rationed. Anthony Heath, professor of sociology at Oxford, says, 'What's declining is the discrepancy in social background between fathers and sons.' In a society where conventional wisdom bemoans the decline of families and the impotence of parents, family matters more than it has for many, many years. 'When I gave a lecture recently, I asked how many students were the first generation to get into higher education. Hardly any were. Whereas when I was a student in the 1960s most of our parents had not been to university.'

Think of a game of musical chairs where there are as many seats as players. Only if someone vacates the chair do you get a place. As John Goldthorpe of Nuffield College, Oxford, puts it ruthlessly: 'Downward mobility must be promoted to exactly the same extent as upwards because fluidity effects are by their nature symmetrical.'[2] That may mean admissions tutors placing a premium on the applicant whose parents never went to university, and that is a hard message for parents and politicians. Ministers prefer to talk about opportunity as if there could never be losers.

The likelihood of moving up depends, no surprise, on money. Being poor when you are a teenager has profoundly depressing lifetime consequences. In these critical years exams have to be passed and decisions made about whether to go on to further education. An adult who was a poor teenager continues to be at higher risk of poverty as they move into their middle age, even if they were out of poverty in their thirties. Prospects for poor teenagers worsened between the 1970s and the 1980s. Being poor as a teenager in the 1980s nearly quadrupled the odds of

115

being poor as a thirty-year-old in 2000. By the 1980s, being poor as a teenager seems to have played an increasingly important role in predicting poverty in later life. Poverty in the teen years usually means lower qualifications, leading to worse jobs and poorer health in later years – and this 'lock in' factor may be growing.[3]

Encouraging these bright Brent students to aim higher is a good cause, and teachers and schools can make a difference to their students' lives, but many of their peers' destinies will have been fixed much younger. Exams at sixteen are a great barrier: most of those who leap that hurdle will go on to take A-levels. But here are the odds: 77% of English middle-class children get five good GCSEs, while only 32% of working-class children make the grade. Generally speaking, how well they do at school is closely related to how much their parents earn. Most will sail through key stage three at age fourteen if their mother and father's combined income is over £30,000. There is a fair probability that children with family incomes below £20,000 are going to struggle.

For those who do jump the age-sixteen hurdle, the social class they come from will make a little less difference thereafter. Most who get five GCSEs will get at least two A-level passes, and even two bad passes will take them on to a university somewhere. Nine out of ten who get a minimum of two A-levels go on to university. Only 19% of the A-level passers come from lower-income backgrounds, against 43% from better-off backgrounds.

The UK, conventional wisdom used to say, would become more meritocratic as it modernized; the glittering prizes should go to those who proved their worth in fair and neutral exams. Michael Young, who coined the term 'meritocracy' in the 1950s, used it as a satirical warning, fearing that the connection between ability and job was growing and would become a stranglehold, creating a new class system based on exam-passing and formal attainment. His fears were misplaced. It's background not ability that rules economic opportunity. At all levels of ability, parents' social class is closely correlated with whether students stay on, take exams and scramble up the educational ladder. According to John Goldthorpe and colleagues, 'There is little reason to suppose that over the last quarter century academic ability became of any greater importance relative to class background in determining the probability of students continuing to A-level.'[4] There is little reason to believe 'that educational qualifications are becoming increasingly dominant in processes of social selection'. Instead, those qualifications are far more likely to be a sign of where you came from in the first place.

Class may even be growing in importance at job interviews. Employers pay attention to exam passes, but rate other factors highly as well – and those could have a lot to do with class and social background, with the manner and self-confidence that comes with pedigree. A degree matters: if you get one, you have a 90% chance of getting a job in the upper echelons of the labour market, regardless of where you came from in the social pecking order. That hasn't changed.

Parents' affluence and education are strong predictors of what happens to their children in all countries, but the relationship is particularly strong in the UK. The same international

evidence suggests, and not just in Sweden, that early-years programmes and extended schooling can reduce the pull of parental
culture and money.[5] In that Nordic country, children are more
likely to succeed or fail at school on the basis of their own
talents and inclinations rather than their parents' social class.
That seems to be for two reasons. Firstly, Sweden is more equal
from top to bottom, so the quality of life in the social classes is
less distinct; wherever the distance between top and bottom
is least, the movement between classes is greatest. And secondly,
education has a more direct impact on children's lives in Sweden
because over the decades more has been spent on schools from
the earliest age onwards.

Social injustice – class – is a touchy subject in a society where
we supposedly no longer defer to rank or breeding, where we
like to imagine merit is all and fierce competition for reward
drives the economy. The well off need to believe they earned
their success by hard work at school and university. It's the sociological equivalent of a rom-com tale of the boardroom
magnate falling for the waitress or a Catherine Cookson rags-
to-riches yarn – but statistically, these are fairy tales. Along with
poor job mobility, people are increasingly less likely to marry
outside their own social milieu and income bracket. Sociologists
call our propensity to share our lives with those fundamentally
similar to ourselves 'assortative mating'. True love has coexisted
for many hundreds of years with the preservation and transmission of privilege. A few brave souls have always crossed the
class divide to find their heart's desire, but for most of human-
kind, when it comes to coupling, socio-economic similarity
takes precedence. Knights court ladies, while swineherds steal

away with shepherdesses. Seduce outside your class, but Don Giovanni was never going to marry Zerlina.

A paper from the Institute for Social and Economic Research at the University of Essex says the incomes and jobs of parents closely match those of both their children and the people their children marry or cohabit with – and that the match is growing.[6] For the cohort born in 1970, the ratio between the son's parents' money and his wife's earnings turned out about the same as between the income of the daughter's parents and what her husband earns. It's as if sons are pre-selecting their partners on the grounds of their parents' income and, as the researchers put it, 'marriage is now an important route through which economic status persists for men, as has long been considered the case for women'. This effect grew during the 1980s and 1990s and it is bound up with falling class mobility. No one suggests these changes play out consciously, but sons appear to be striving to find another way of insulating themselves against falling down the ladder, and young women of similar status are the solution.

The great hope was that a rapid expansion of university places, first under the Conservatives and then under Labour, would in itself boost social mobility and draw in young people from poorer backgrounds. This painless version was espoused by Tony Blair and Gordon Brown, underpinning their target of expanding university enrolment to half the eighteen to twenty-five age cohort. In 1975, 5.6% of UK men had a degree. By 2000 this had more than trebled to 17.9%. For women the rise was even steeper, from 2.3% to 15.3%. The proportion of those graduating from the poorest backgrounds rose too – but only from 5% in the early 1980s to about 9% in the mid-1990s. It was the richer groups in society who seized the new places, many of them middle-class girls who in previous generations had been prevented from joining their brothers at university. University became, in the words of the minister Margaret Hodge, a middle-class right but a working-class privilege.

The irony is that increasing university places may actually have widened the qualification gaps between rich and poor children. In the late 1960s, the heady days of student protest, roughly 27% of children from middle and upper backgrounds went to university, but only 4% from working-class and unskilled homes. By the twenty-first century, working-class participation has risen to 18%. That is social progress. But the number of better-off pupils going on to university has risen by much more, to 48%. More university places may be a social good in itself, but as a vehicle for social mobility expansion may come to be seen as a failure. And while students from low-income homes may go to college in increasing numbers – the students from Brent among them – they attend lower-ranking institutions leading to lower-income jobs. As having a degree is now more ordinary, their position relative to the top may remain pretty much the same.

There are green shoots of progress. In February 2008 AimHigher was given £74.1 million for another three years, with the target of showing by 2011 that the programme had 'contributed to narrowing the social class gap'. Schools improve, and raise their students' chances. Some children do win against the odds: two of the boys on that visit to Oxford got stunning GCSE results. Izatullah Haleghi got fifteen GCSE passes, eight of them As. Jameel Shah, the boy who had escaped death in Afghanistan and arrived here at the age of thirteen, speaking not a word of English, passed fourteen GCSEs with eight A*s and six As. Of the Capital City Academy exam cohort, 24% gained five A–C grades (including the key subjects of English and maths). That was up from 11% two years ago. Some 53% got five A–C GCSEs (though not necessarily including both English and maths) and that was up from 16% two years before. Given the resources and the determination, schools can improve, even in hard-pressed areas such as Brent. But in this unequal society the effects of such improvement are inherently constrained.

PART THREE

Just Rewards: The policies that work

CHAPTER 7

A sure start for children

The well off protest that they are willing to pay tax and might even pay more, if only. If only they were confident that government wasn't wasteful, if only the state would spend it well, if only public officials were more competent and reliable. People need a get-out clause and their repeated argument against tax is that money falls into a bureaucratic black hole somewhere between the intention to do good and the actual delivery. In his report to the Treasury on efficiency, the former head of the Office of Government Commerce, Sir Peter Gershon, gave them some ammunition: not enough ends up providing a public service, too much is consumed in processes and procedures.[1] But Sir John Bourn, the former Comptroller and Auditor General, noted that in assessing performance 'a much brighter spotlight is shone on public as opposed to private sector delivery'. Objective evaluations of the effectiveness of government schemes are drowned in the cacophony of noise from the media, eager to find public waste and ignorant about how to find the far more opaque wastage hidden within the private sector. For much of the twentieth century the UK's newspapers were skewed right: the Northcliffes, Beaverbrooks and Murdochs were dedicated to a maverick brand of anti-collectivism. Sometimes authoritarian in tone, sometimes almost anarchic, the message is still consistent: the state is over-mighty and ineffective. Taxes are wasted and, as Mrs Thatcher kept saying, citizens will always spend the pound in their pocket better than government could ever do. In debates about health and education, the worst examples grab the headlines, the rest too often silence. In the *Daily Mail*'s lexicon, 'social engineering' (its term for promoting social mobility) is an offence against the natural order and doomed to fail.

Improving the life chances of poor children is difficult and expensive. No hard and fast formula prescribes precisely how much it would take in cash benefits, credits and family financial support on the one side and public services, especially early-years schemes and schools, on the other. Labour's child-poverty target is reachable through the redistribution of cash but sustainable only through long-term social and educational programmes. Some will fail, others won't deliver for decades. But the intellectual basis for intervention is robust. In this arena, government works. We can change social destiny, if there is the political will and popular assent for the tax to fund it.

To see what can be done, visit the Sure Start Children's Centre in Bellingham in south-west London and talk to Shirley Mucklow. She is one of the matriarchs who helped set it up in

2000, and who helps run one of the first examples of this pioneering programme, her own two grandchildren with special needs among the beneficiaries.

Here is an example of public spending helping local people take responsibility for changing their own lives. Thanks to the centre, the 600 babies and toddlers growing up in this ward have a better chance than ever before. Sure Start is the jewel in the crown of Labour's social policy, the missing link in the welfare state's promise of cradle-to-grave assistance. Rolling out in every neighbourhood, starting in the most deprived, new children's centres are becoming a hub for local communities, a meeting place for young families, where young lives may be turned around before it's too late. Here, ideally, are sited all the services a family might need, from midwives to training programmes helping mothers find jobs, from speech therapy for small children to debt advice, from tai chi classes and parenting support to childcare, cafés, chatting and fun.

Monitoring reports show the potential of children's centres in changing lives.[2] Comparing 9,000 three-year-olds across 150 Sure Start areas with children in similar areas without Sure Start, evaluators found 'parents showed less negative parenting and a better home learning environment ... Three-year-olds had better social development with higher levels of positive social behaviour and independence than children in similar areas not having a programme.' Three-year-old children in Sure Start areas had higher immunization rates and fewer accidental injuries. An earlier evaluation, in 2005, had suggested that Sure Start was not reaching the neediest and most problematic families, those like Callum's which stand to gain most from improved parenting. Sure Start now reaches nearly all children in its areas, but this is a programme in its infancy, still training staff. The budgeted cost of Sure Start plus nursery places was £4.4 billion in 2007–8, up from £1.1 billion in 1996–7.

Bellingham's transformation is astonishing. A before-and-after visitor would be shocked at how much better the park, shops, streets – the very air of the place – feel. At the southern end of the London borough of Lewisham, Bellingham is a poor place with high unemployment. White working-class families have lived here for generations, many since the brick-and-pebbledash council estate was built by the London County Council in the 1930s. Once, as across much of the old LCC, a 'sons and daughters' lettings policy gave the estate's own children a priority call on homes; it was replaced during the 1980s by assessment of socio-economic need. Bellingham was a community of sorts, but one without much pride or capacity to look after itself on its own.

The area's streets are built as a grid radiating out from a small central park which had long since gone to seed, a barren dump of scrubland for needles and condoms where local bullies intimidated anyone foolish enough to enter their terrain. The British National Party and Combat 18 had a grip on a couple of the local pubs. Until recently it was a semi-derelict place, forgotten by time and policy, with failing schools.

Shirley Mucklow was born and bred here, a mainstay of the tenants association, the only community action until 2000. Bellingham was chosen for an early Sure Start scheme because it was Lewisham's worst ward on all socio-economic indicators.

A sure start for children

For once, it was lucky to be worst, for Sure Start has had a gal-vanic effect. Sure Start puts its hope, its money and its focus into the beginning of children's lives, when it is easiest to interrupt cycles of deprivation, where you can catch babies early and attract mothers who yearn for somewhere to go in the long days of caring for toddlers alone. As the evidence shows, inter-vention has to be early and fast: lack of love, talk and stimulation can destroy. It's never too late, but after the age of two everything is remedial.

Together with a local church minister, Shirley and a group of mothers seized the chance to shape the programme themselves. 'I was called the community development manager, but at first my office was the arm of my settee.' First they took over a derelict shop front in a local parade so full of empty properties it used to look like an aged mouth with missing teeth. Since then, Sure Start has taken over a couple of others, breathing new life into the whole row, attracting new shops and even, to Shirley's amazement, an estate agent, who has just moved in. A programme designed for babies has turned into an engine for regeneration that is transforming Bellingham.

The founders needed a quick win to prove to sceptical Bellingham locals that this was not just yet another under-funded, half-hearted renewal plan that would run out of money before the paint on the signboard had dried. The mothers iden-tified the park, that eyesore at the hub of the estate, as needing attention first. Early cash was spent on building a bright tod-dlers' playground there, which has a drop-in nursery attached for wet weather, staffed all day long by people who play with young children, but whose main purpose is to lure new parents into joining Sure Start's activities and using its services. On one side of the park there now is an all-weather football pitch and a vandal-proof shelter for adolescents to hang out. Residents have started to stop and chat, watching the children at play. The grass is well kept, the playground unvandalized, and there is a garden where elderly residents sit. CCTV cameras have helped curb vandalism, but mainly the all-age use of the common space transformed the park. Staff are in the playground all day and teenagers have a corner of their own. This cared-for piece of ground commands common respect and was the first sign of a community reawakening.

Next the team built a specially designed Sure Start centre, and a new nursery for sixty-five children run by a non-profit company where any parents can bring children to play, with music days and messy-play days. The team buy in NHS services, among them a midwife, health visitors, speech and language assistance and a children's mental-health therapist. One in four of the children here was in need of some kind of therapy.

The mothers speak with one voice: this is the place to be. There is a café to linger in and help is always on hand, a life-saver to many with often little else in their lives. It is a one-stop shop for struggling families whose problems range from domestic violence to dealing with council-tax benefit. The centre offers IT training and a Jobcentre Plus for parents who want to go back to work, with free English lessons for those who need them. A fathers' group has been convened and inside one of the shop fronts in the parade is a sensory centre, where parents can bring seriously disturbed and disabled children for calming sessions – with music, lights, books and big cushions.

For parents of disabled children, often the most isolated, staff from the home education service visit to offer help, support and stimulation.

Sure Start's success rests on the involvement of parents. They take a third of seats on the board, which administers a budget of £875,000 a year. From the earliest days Shirley and the other mothers made a ritual of a free community lunch once a month, cooked by the parents together. The mothers now exert a political muscle that this ward certainly never had before. They have persuaded the council to build a leisure centre nearby with sports and activities for older children and adults. A new tent-shaped youth centre has just opened in the grounds, with an extra nursery attached. You get the picture – here are stunning new buildings, an area transformed, streets reclaimed, neighbourhood wardens on patrol and a community of parents who know each other well and will work together as their children progress through local schools. Parents who used to be isolated strangers come together, bringing their babies and small children, and find here life-changing experiences they never imagined. Lindsay Hall, an evaluator of Sure Start from the Anglia Polytechnic University, put her finger on it: 'Mums look different. They are more confident.'

Perhaps, if Callum's mother came to a Bellingham-style Sure Start, she might not find herself alone and angry with her child every day. She might find herself new friends and advice that could change the way she treats him. Learning about what small children need, learning to talk and hug and listen and encourage, she might change how she felt just enough to save Callum from the worst emotional neglect.

But Sure Start is by no means only for the dysfunctional and distressed. All mothers have anxieties, feel lonely and need to be with others. Take Karen, who had her first child before Bellingham's Sure Start opened, and the second afterwards. 'There's no comparison. Having my first child was a lonely experience, my husband out at work long hours, and I had distant and changing health visitors and no relationship with any of them. Suddenly this whole area really changed, with this friendly place with a lot of other mothers instead of being alone all day. To have a midwife from Sure Start right from the beginning of your pregnancy until the end, that's wonderful. My health visitor has helped me with behaviour problems with my youngest, and she's always there, always on her mobile.' Karen has joined the Sure Start board and thanks to its IT training now works part-time as a school librarian.

Everyone who visits comes away amazed, especially those of us who knew the area seven years ago. Every neighbourhood needs a children's centre as good as this. Health visitors attend every child born on the estate and entice the families into the centre to link up with other new parents. Problems are more likely to be spotted quickly – drugs, drink, post-natal depression, mental illness, domestic violence, poor English, things that put a family at risk. Here is the welfare state for the earliest stages in children's lives, at last.

But no one says it's done and dusted. Improvements are bound to be incremental, generation by generation. Some families resist intrusion. Others in deep trouble are too ashamed to mix with ordinary families. Curing alcoholism or curbing violence is difficult. Children from desperate families may never be good parents themselves and the shortage of affordable housing, especially in London and the cities, means many are on the move, never staying long enough to get enough help. Bellingham's ethnic composition has been changing, as housing is found for asylum seekers and migrants. Once mainly white, nearly half of Bellingham's residents are now ethnic minority. Families are often placed in temporary accommodation and then move on, so there is now a staggering 40%-a-year turnover of families in the area. Settling these children into any kind of programme, let alone measuring the programme's true success, becomes very difficult.

Sure Start got going when the Labour government's mania for targets was at its height. Hoping for quick, showy results, ministers ordered evaluations way too early. They focused on inputs, not outcomes. Performance data insisted upon by the Department for Education and Skills was meaningless: Bellingham got a black mark because only 12% of children registered with Sure Start are active members of a public library, a daft target when the estate has no library, although the board are campaigning for one. Patience from policy makers is required, as Sure Start's strongest effects may emerge over decades. Results for a similar American programme, part of President Johnson's Head Start called Perry High/Scope, were phenomenal, but they took a long time to show up. Two socially identical sets of children were followed into adulthood, after being put through an intensive pre-school programme, with home visits to help support mothers; the control group were given no extra help. The effects lasted a lifetime: by the age of thirty, the deprived children who had intensive help in the early years were doing far better than peers who had not been on the programme. Those crucial two years seemed to protect them in later life. Fewer lived on social security, committed crime, suffered mental illness, or went to prison. Many more had jobs and owned their own homes compared with the control group. These American children, mostly from problem families, didn't necessarily grow up to become academic high-flyers or move into high-paying jobs, but they did better than they would have done. The programme that made their mothers better, gentler parents seemed to give the children the soft social skills of communication and empathy that in time rescued them from failure and social isolation.

One danger for Sure Start is that the government is spreading the programme too thinly. Some 3,500 children's centres are to open by 2010, an ambition that, on present budgets, means many will be not be purpose-built like Bellingham. There may not be the money for expert midwives, health visitors, speech and mental-health therapists who can make such a difference to families in trouble. They may be housed mostly in corners of primary schools, and some mothers Sure Start most needs to reach may be deterred, thanks to their own bad memories of school.

Sure Start's greatest lack is enough free crèche places for families on the edge. Child tax credits partly pay for childcare, but are available only to families in work. Many of the neediest children come from chaotic families who are not in work and may never be: the children of alcoholics, drug users and depressives who most need to be looked after in stimulating surroundings. Embracing these 'hardest to reach' would be easier with an offer of some hours of free childcare.

It's not perfect and by no means universal yet – Labour hopes all under-fives will have access to Sure Start by 2010. But already, here is a shining example of a social intervention worth the money, which justifies the taxation that pays for it and refutes those who claim any extra taxation would simply be wasted. Yet it is also illustrates how badly the public case is made for social spending and the redistributive taxation necessary to support it. The UK spends 0.5% of GDP on under-fives, while France spends twice as much at 1% and Denmark spends 2%. That mirrors their relative success in both greater equality and more social mobility.

Ministers were fearful, unimaginative, perhaps gender-bound – male politicians still nonplussed by mothers and babies. The programme wasn't ever sold to the voters and few except its users know anything about this Labour triumph. Tony Blair never quite saw political mileage in it, and Brown talks about it only to those who already know – never to the City or high earners or others who need to know. Conservatives have eyed the costs critically, hinting that pre-school is something mothers should do, nothing to do with the state. David Cameron has been dismissive and one of his shadow ministers, David Willetts, even suggested Sure Start threatened playgroups and private nurseries. So this programme has by no means yet entered the nation's bloodstream as a well-loved and essential part of the welfare state, as firmly rooted and unquestioned as the NHS or primary schools. But it is getting there. If spending priorities hold and there are no cataclysmic changes in policy, Sure Start's 'graduates' will move through the schools and eventually the colleges, demonstrating its worth in the way they behave and what they achieve.

CHAPTER 8

Newall Green

In primary schools up and down the country miniature coats hang on hooks, posters adorn the classroom and a heady mix of fear and delight at this new experience is palpable. On one table squirm the bright sparks who can write their names, who know their letters, can count to twenty and sing nursery rhymes. They are eager to listen to stories and quick to answer whenever the teacher asks a question. On the slow table rattle the children who can't sit still, don't listen, can barely speak, can't even hold a pencil. Some have little concept that the hieroglyphics written in books can magically transform themselves into stories in the head. On day one of primary school, a child's language is crucial to their success. If there are problems now it's nearly too late and twelve – soon to be fourteen – years of compulsory schooling stretch ahead.

Just Rewards: The policies that work

For those stranded at square one government-funded supplementary education offers a last chance. Here is another answer to doubters who claim the state is an intrusion, a waster that doesn't deserve their tax money. Come to Wythenshawe in Manchester, to Newall Green Primary. This school faces a welter of social problems but it's on the up and up, showing that background can be bested and deprivation in those critical early years can be compensated for. Parental background remains the primary determinant of how well the children will do, but every little bit of mitigation helps.

A large single-storey 1960s building surrounded by bare green space, Newall Green Primary is set in the middle of one of Europe's largest housing estates. This is mostly poor white territory. It is one of those sprawling post-war estates of suburban housing with well-intended but unused grass verges stretching for miles. Nearby Manchester airport brings in shift-work jobs, but drugs, drink and high unemployment are endemic, say the teachers, as they strive to give children the love, attention and care that many lack at home.

A few minutes before we arrived, the headteacher Richard Lait had called the police to deal with a regular problem: a former pupil lurking in the grounds. The boy had recently left a young offenders' institution – the only further education he is likely to get – and had been spotted eyeing up school equipment, probably planning to sneak in and grab a laptop to pay for drugs. One teacher murmured that he'd soon be back, but the next time probably as one of their new parents.

In Wythenshawe most children come from normal families, but the area also has a disproportionate share of families in no condition to bring up children, parents who themselves came from barely functioning families. Children see routine violence at home and imitate it at school. One father attacked an education welfare officer with a machete and another is an often-arrested Manchester City football hooligan. 'We have a lot of attention-deficit-hyperactivity-disordered children, and a lot on Ritalin.' Ritalin is essentially a drug for the deprived. It is prescribed to mitigate attention deficit hyperactivity disorder (ADHD), which is more prevalent in boys from hard backgrounds. The ADHD risk factors are: low social class, large family size, severe marital discord, paternal criminality, maternal mental disorder and foster placement.[1]

Wythenshawe is the kind of place a documentary crew would choose to depict struggle and deprivation. In television, voyeurism is fashionable, as is the view that nothing can be done in the social badlands. Fence them in, give them an ASBO, tag and curfew, then safely ignore them until the next titillating peek brought by the next thrill-seeking television show. Class mockery is entertainment, from *The Jeremy Kyle Show* to *Wife Swap*, and a score more shows that parade the dim and desperate. Here is a view of the world that encourages belief in a fixed 'underclass', Huxley's Morlocks, mad and bad.

Class continuity is strong. On day one in the nursery a child is assigned a table according to their development and ability, a table on which they may stay throughout school – and even throughout life. Three-year-olds arrive who can barely speak and children are sometimes still in nappies. Embarrassed mothers whip them off at the door but it soon becomes all too obvious the children aren't potty-trained. Wythenshawe has no Sure Start children's centre. The nursery head says it would make all the difference. 'Years ago at least every child was checked regularly by health visitors, but that's stopped now. There is no three-year-old check. I get children arriving here with quite serious cerebral palsy and other glaringly obvious disabilities that no one has picked up. A lot have chronic glue ear and they can't hear at all. Some of these young parents just have no idea what's normal and they don't notice anything abnormal about their child's development. It's very late to wait for diagnosis by the time they arrive on our doorstep.' The best Sure Starts have health visitors who go into every home with a new baby to check on young children and advise families. There are precious few health visitors in Wythenshawe.

School cannot undo the effects of background or absence of help in the early years, but it can compensate, or at least stop disadvantage snowballing. Newall Green is a good school. When Richard Lait first arrived as head in 2003 he recalls the mayhem. Children were charging up and down corridors shouting and hitting each other; classrooms were loud and unruly. 'The worst was dinner time and the break afterwards was horrible. I was terrified that if inspectors walked through that front door they'd have shut the place down right away.' It is a big primary with over 700 children, hard to keep in order. It is easy to lose sight of the many quiet children who cause no trouble but silently fall further and further behind. 'It took two years to get the place vaguely human,' Lait says, 'and some kids from violent backgrounds still suddenly kick off unpredictably, but we can handle it now.'

A knock interrupted us, and a nine-year-old put her head

round the door. Lait smiled and beckoned her in. She entered triumphantly, waving a collage in the air with a great grin. Good work is brought to the head for praise, which he duly lavished. 'That's it, that's what works, encouragement.' Children who get a set number of stickers or stars are given a letter to take home to say how well they have done, letters that are sometimes framed or displayed on the fridge. 'It's easy to forget to encourage the ordinary kids, and spend all your time on the ones in trouble. Rewards work.' So does the school's therapeutic room, staffed all day by two classroom assistants who see children with problems. In one corner is a hollowed-out papier-mâché tree. When children are miserable or out of control they can choose to sit inside its trunk to calm down, and they like it in there. The room has signs and pictures about emotions. Disturbed and disruptive children come to talk about their feelings and to stay out of the trouble they might be causing that day. It's a quiet, gentle space, well ordered by warm and grandmotherly assistants who are specially trained for the job. Call it an exclusion zone or sin bin, it's also the school's secret heart. Children like it, eagerly talking in a group about what makes them cry; they are encouraged to listen and respond to each other. Classroom assistants can't provide these children with the professional therapy many need, but it works for the school. Classrooms are quiet, their doors standing open on to quiet corridors in an atmosphere of peace.

In 2006 Ofsted rated Newall Green satisfactory for every-thing and good in some areas. 'That's a miracle, I can assure you,' says the head. His deputy, who has been here longer, nods her strong agreement. We had been puzzled why this particular primary had been recommended to us as an example of what investment can do – a judgement of 'satisfactory' doesn't sound fulsome. But satisfactory in Wythenshawe is much more than it sounds. Surviving, let alone making giant strides forwards, in a place like this is a formidable achievement: public money has been effectively spent. Remember too that Ofsted keeps putting up the bar as schools improve: this might well have rated 'good' a decade ago. Many such schools have been turned around in the toughest circumstances – children rescued from the certainty of failure and given a chance. Teachers and heads are not miracle workers and the children's social circumstances can sometimes be too strong to overcome. But it is never too late to deploy more effort, more hard work in classroom and corridor, more highly skilled expertise. And a lot more money.

Compared with ten years ago there are half as many schools classed as failing – 2.9% now – despite Ofsted rightly raising standards. The Blair–Brown government invested heavily and teaching is a better-paid and more popular profession. Salary levels recognize the difference a good head makes and there are fewer vacancies for this critical role. But how much further Britain still has to go. It will take years of spending at high pitch before results work their way all through the system, so that children entering primaries such as Newall Green feel the effect for their entire school life.

Newall Green is also a pilot 'extended' school. Extended schools offer clubs and activities before and after school hours, childcare outside the school day and an open-door policy for the local community to use the school's equipment for adult classes in sport, art and IT. Extended schools will refer children to clinics or to specialist help. Here at last is a serious attempt to join up education with health, social services, benefits, employment and debt-advice services. Newall Green now provides breakfast and tea, its doors open from 8 a.m. to 6 p.m. to allow parents to work and to give children extra time for homework, reading, sport or just fun and friendship. Most mothers work part-time, so few use the full opening hours, but about fifty children turn up for breakfast every morning, paying 50p for a decent meal. Many never get breakfast at home and the school found behaviour improved once children stopped coming to class hungry. Some teachers arrive early to give extra reading lessons before school starts, while others chat and play with the children. The day starts with friendliness and warmth, encouraging more children to arrive early instead of late.

After school and all through the holidays a club run as a separate business by one of the dinner ladies employs specialist staff who offer arts, crafts, drama and sport. Attendance costs £5 a day, and parents with jobs are reimbursed through their childcare tax credits. Extended schools will offer pupils from poorer backgrounds the same out-of-school activities that middle-class children take for granted – sport, dancing, judo, drama, ballet and music lessons – although the activities on offer are still a long way from the round of private classes middle-class children enjoy, and they do have to pay, which will always deter the families needing it most.

When Lait arrived at Newall Green a large sign on the door told parents to wait outside in the playground. Now they are not just welcomed but every ploy is used to tug them in. One programme offers parents with literacy difficulties extra lessons in reading and arithmetic after school, sitting alongside their children and learning together to mutual benefit. If they complete all the sessions, the family gets a free holiday in the Lake District. Education and parenting advice workshops are thinly disguised as activity evenings. Teachers are trained to help parents who are struggling with their children's behaviour. 'Many are keen to learn strategies for coping because they know all too well that if they are having trouble controlling their children at seven, they have no hope when children reach fourteen,' the head says. 'But it takes more than that. It needs home visits and follow-up sessions.' Families that live chaotically with no set bedtimes or regular meals can't suddenly snap into orderly systems with their out-of-control children. 'How do you get parents to remember to take their children at the right time to an appointment in two weeks' time with a therapist or doctor two bus rides away when they've never had a calendar or a diary in the house?'

None of this is easy. Results are slow and failure and backsliding inevitable. But those are not arguments against investment, merely against impatience. Joining up services is easy on paper, but hard in life. Stretched local authority social workers tend to focus on children in immediate danger of physical violence, so Newall Green together with the local secondary school hired their own social worker and school nurse.

The greatest need, the head says, is for expert speech and language therapy at the school, not in a clinic far away. Professional therapy can make all the difference for children who can't talk in sentences. Unless they can make sense of distinct separate words they will never learn even the basic concept of reading. In 2007 Manchester City Council told schools they could refer two children at a time but Newall Green reckons a third of its pupils need help. Some classroom assistants have been given speech and language training but no one pretends this substitutes for the professional help these children need.

Extended schools rest on an inspiring, optimistic vision. Labour's 2003 Green Paper *Every Child Matters* promised, along with family support, a new unity among policies and departments dealing with children, more joining up of school and social services. Some heads still resist working with social care, especially in academically high-scoring schools, so the extended schools remain a partial sketch. Nothing like enough money yet supports them and most families have to pay for out-of-hours activities. Not for the first time Labour pledged Scandinavian outcomes on American spending levels. Youth crime is a problem but the solution has to lie in early years and primary schools. The TaxPayers' Alliance should be up in arms about the shortage of cash for therapy: a few pounds spent earlier would save hundreds of thousands on crime, social benefits and mental-hospital admissions.

Schooling is a rich and complex business. To educate all children to the best of their ability is an extraordinary task in its breadth and diversity: from nursery to university; the child in care; the Polish speaker; the one with learning difficulties; the high-flyer. Visitors to Newall Green are left optimistic, but also chastened. How effective can schools ever be? Dismay

greeted the negative headlines following a study of their efficiency.[2] But alongside the finding that productivity, mainly
measured by exam passes per pound spent on teachers and
equipment, might even have been falling in recent years, the
statisticians acknowledged 'there are many education outcomes for which there is currently no quality adjustment
factor'.

Such adjustments might include the happiness of school-
children; their behaviour; the integration of schools into their
communities; whether teachers, with a bit more time, are
organizing more clubs or becoming more active participants in
local affairs. How do you measure a child's sense that education matters because a school is well cared for? The proportion
of young people committing crimes has fallen, which may or
may not have something to do with better schools. Should the
Office for National Statistics measurement take in the fact that
since the 1990s teaching has moved from fifty-fourth to a place
in the top ten favoured graduate occupations? Investment in
school buildings has repaired the decay of decades; there are
fewer leaking roofs; gone are the outside toilets and the tatty
1970s sets of books shared one to three pupils.

Too often there is a lack of balance – or plain common
sense – in the obsessive monitoring of sensitive services and
programmes, and sometimes the search for failure is malicious.
Of course interventions must be based on evidence accumulated from trials and studies. One was going on at Newall
Green, a programme that turned out to be a compelling example of what can be done given enough money and political will.
Every Child a Reader is a story of potential transformations.

Newall Green

The most important duty of primary schools is to make sure that every child can read before moving on to secondary school, yet 20% leave below the eleven-year-old standard, some illiterate. Without reading these children's secondary years will drift by in a fog of incomprehension. No wonder children who can't read end up as permanent truants – lessons make no sense to them. High proportions of the unemployed and prison inmates can't read. Illiteracy is like blindness or deafness, where everyone else communicates in a foreign tongue. Over a million citizens cannot read and every year some 35,000 illiterate children leave primary school in England to join those ranks, nearly one in ten of all eleven-year-old boys. The government tries hard to repair decades of damage with its £3 billion Skills for Life programme to give adults basic reading and numeracy.

Everyone knows that catching them young is a better answer. Every Child a Reader is aimed at five- and six-year-olds who have made no progress in learning to read after their first year at school. Using specially trained teachers, the scheme offers the weakest pupils intensive one-to-one teaching for half an hour every day for up to twenty weeks, using a highly structured reading recovery programme. It works because it involves parents as well. Every evening children take home a new book to read and a set of cards that make a sentence.

Applied and tested first in the 2005–6 school year, the innovation had remarkable results.[3] Children on it were compared with an identical group with the same social characteristics and the same initial reading standards. Some 63% of the worst readers were boys and 58% of them were on free school meals, demonstrating (not for the first time) the strength of the connection between home and school under-attainment. After four months evaluators found children on the scheme gaining twenty-one months in terms of measured reading ability, well over four times the normal rate of progress. During the same period children in the control group fell further behind in their classes, all too predictably. Reading recovery successfully lifted eight out of ten of these lowest-achieving six-year-olds up to reach the appropriate reading age. All the evidence from previous pilots shows that children don't slip back, keeping their reading skills throughout the rest of their education. The scheme has since been rolled out at other schools, including Manchester's.

Mary is in council care and living with foster parents. In her first year at Newall Green school she was often late or missed days altogether and plainly had emotional problems. One report said that 'Mary's greatest difficulty lies with understanding the language of books'. She barely grasped that letters put together hold messages. She confused letters and couldn't understand the concept of the beginning of a sentence. She had only managed to write a two-letter word.

When we visited, after fourteen weeks of reading recovery with half an hour a day intensive one-to-one tuition, she had made startling progress and was at a slightly higher level than average for her class, spelling and writing words with several syllables. Without help Mary could read her lines for her part in the Christmas play. Her classroom teacher says she is a changed child, confident, eager to join in, keen to read and write. She is no longer isolated, withdrawn or reluctant.

Newall Green

There's Jim, a tiny, frail little boy, nervy, with a shaven head, still at the early stages of the programme. His teacher said he had been hopelessly lost, but here he was finding his way. He was hugely proud of the very first book he had read, keen to take it home and show his mother, keen to get on to the next and then the next. We could see right there, before our eyes, a child whose fate was being changed. What is that worth? No one who sat in that room could do anything but conclude here was a programme well worth the investment.

In the 2007 budget Gordon Brown announced that the Every Child a Reader pilot scheme was proving such a success that it would be rolled out to the 6% of five- and six-year-old children in England, 35,000 in all, who struggle in their first reading years and are destined to leave primary unable to read.

The Institute of Education found that over three quarters of the hardest to teach children were restored to average or above-average literacy standards after thirty-eight hours of one-to-one teaching. Their motivation, behaviour and work habits improved significantly. So did their emotional health and well-being, their support for others and their aspirations. By pulling up the ones at the back of the class, the average reading age for the whole class rose. Remarkably, Every Child a Reader would never have got off the ground if KPMG and other charitable foundations had not backed it and put in a rigorous academic evaluation. Why did it take the intervention of a charity to validate such a scheme? The answer seems to be money. At Newall Green only four children at a time were on the scheme in 2007, rising to eight in 2008. We asked the head how many needed it and he thought about sixteen children a year. This number showed the scale of the gap and gives a glimpse of the potential. Next time you hear someone saying tax money goes to waste, arguing against the better off paying more, remember Mary and Jim and all the children who are yet to be helped.

CHAPTER 9

Worthwhile work

Debbie is a bright thirty-year-old, a fanatic about keeping fit, who never expected to go near a benefit office. But life sometimes takes a wrong turn. She had a management job with prospects, but when her partner left she found herself alone with a young child and couldn't juggle both. 'I wanted better training, but the Jobcentre could only offer me a low-level vocational course. I'm way above that level but I couldn't possibly afford the cost of paying for a course for myself. So I just took the first job they gave me to get off the dole, working in Tesco.' The job meant travelling every day between Southend and Barking. After paying fares she wasn't earning any more at work than she was getting on income support. When her son was ill for a month the journey was impossible and she gave up the job.

Debbie was lucky enough to be in the right area to be offered a place on an innovative experiment being tried by the Department of Work and Pensions called Employment, Retention and Advancement (ERA). It was an experiment in taking people in low-level jobs and giving them the where-withal, including the aspiration, to move on and up. Debbie cannot thank ERA enough. 'It changed my life. It put me on my feet.' She talks about her personal adviser, Anita, as a real friend and saviour. 'She was always there for me.'

The scheme paid for driving lessons and the cost of a nursery place for Debbie's son. With Anita, she worked out an employment plan and the training courses she needed were paid for. Now she has a company of her own training security guards for the NHS, teaching them conflict management techniques and physical methods of controlling violence: she has contracts stretching into the far future. She has bought a car, her life is in order and her childcare is secure. She pays taxes, so money spent on the ERA programme pays back handsomely: Debbie will add to the nation's GDP for the rest of her working life.

Meeting some of the 'advancement support' advisers from the six ERA pilots, we found enthusiastic missionaries for the programme. Civil servants are not given to flights of passion. 'It often brought tears to my eyes,' said one, a hardened Jobcentre Plus official of many years' experience. She spoke of her liberation from working with strict targets that had often obliged her to squeeze square pegs into round holes. Now she had the freedom and resources to match each person with better training and employment. 'So many times clients get into debt, or can't afford something small that would make all the difference to getting work – but on this programme we could help.'

Another said, 'We could look after people. They became my friends, they really did. I'm not looking forward to going back to the huge caseload and the few offers I can make to my usual Jobcentre Plus clients.' One said this: 'You've no idea how satisfying it is to have time with one client to get to the root of their problems and sort them out.'

They talked about a string of case histories. There was the man who had worked as a car valet for years, partly because he could barely read, who seized the chance to do a vocational qualification in childcare followed by further training and then a job as a classroom assistant. Now he is going to train as a teacher. There was the client driving lorries who took a course in falconry. His personal adviser was dubious but the man had a good idea in his head and a plan. It worked: now he does well working on contract to local authorities and companies controlling pigeons in factories and warehouses with his falcons. Another man who was out of work was helped to take a Spanish course. On the strength of it he was able to take up a job offer in Marbella and has moved there with his family. Another woman liked her personal adviser so much she decided to train to become one herself. These are individual trajectories, but routes into work will often be idiosyncratic. ERA shows that the state, in the shape of a dedicated band of advisers, treating people as individuals, can help bridge gaps, change lives and increase productivity. This is a personalized service – and that's why it works.

Labour came to power in 1997 chanting the mantra that work is the best welfare. The party had travelled far since the days when it appeared to put benefits before the obligation to work and on its behalf the economist Richard Layard devised a dynamic New Deal that succeeded in encouraging large numbers of long-term unemployed – especially the young – back to work with personal help, backed by the threat of benefit withdrawal if they failed to take part in programmes and training. Personal advisers offered more help – carrots were offered before sticks. Three quarters of the young unemployed on New Deal programmes graduated into jobs. Here was a win-win for the Treasury and the millions the New Deal helped.

Many New Deal jobs were entry level, using the euphemism borrowed from the US for low-paid work. It implies workers can and will make their way upwards. Getting a job was only the first step, said the chancellor, Gordon Brown. People should be helped to move upwards, to train, improve themselves and get promoted. But the vast majority are going nowhere. Armies of cleaners, carers, caterers, cashiers and clerical workers paid rock-bottom wages cannot all become supervisors and managers. An American study found only 5% of jobs in hotels and catering were 'managerial', and described the 'bleak picture of the almost total lack of upward mobility for most housekeeping and entry level food and beverage workers'.[1] The ladder has limited capacity; most will stay more or less where they are; most will retire from the entry-level jobs they have worked at all their lives.

Yet the work they do is absolutely vital. Civility and good order depend on it. It is work that has to be done well or our hospitals will go uncleaned and old people will be cruelly neglected in care homes. Shelves will go unstacked and orders go unprocessed. As society gets richer, standards and expectations rise and so does the demand for personal services of one kind or another. Who is supposed to do this work and for what level of pay? An endless stream of new immigrants, a slave-class to be kept down? Politicians keep talking about the need to raise aspirations, but who is left to care for the child in the day nursery, to help out in the classroom, playground and school kitchen? Who will clean the streets, patrol the parks and sit at the check-out desk all day?

Many are still stuck without jobs for reasons from personal circumstance to geographic location. People aged over fifty enrol on scheme after scheme, never moving into jobs; they are mostly depressed or unskilled men who fell out of twentieth-century industrial jobs and are too young to qualify for a pension but too old or proud to train for twenty-first-century work. More than 2.5 million are on incapacity benefit, some seriously ill but most too depressed and dispirited to get themselves back into the job market.

They would all be financially and emotionally better off in work but making this employment market work needs government action: people stranded need programmes like ERA, which can be provided by non-profit or private contractors as well. People's lives, their histories, their disappointments and potential don't conform to the economists' statistics, which is why personalized, flexible programmes such as ERA are needed, and should be extended, although the upfront cost may be high.

The New Deal tugged people into low-level jobs where some stayed, but others went round the carousel again, in and out of work and back through New Deal schemes. Sometimes the only jobs they could get were temporary, or dreadful, or just too much to manage. Some people had unresolved problems that made staying in work difficult – especially single mothers relying on unreliable childcare. If they lost a childminder or nursery place they had to leave their jobs.

There must always be second chances, because work is almost universally better for individuals and for society. After its initial success, the New Deal idea is limping, partly because the free training available is limited – National Vocational Qualification (NVQ) level 2, which teaches barely more than basic literacy. Such courses funnel the unemployed into shop, care or office work, where employers don't want ambition or imagination and aspiration evaporates.

ERA is the next step, to tap potential and help people in precarious jobs move up. Because this Rolls-Royce service was set up as a demonstration in a limited number of places, evaluators were able to compare results with what happened to a group of Jobcentre Plus clients who were offered standard New Deal advice and job offers. In the test areas, three groups were eligible for ERA: the unemployed over twenty-five, single parents and those working part-time and drawing working tax credit (which by definition meant they are low paid). The aim for all three groups was to try to get them into better work, to see if they could stay employed and even progress up the career ladder.

Some 16,500 took part. Half of them were randomly removed and received no special help, beyond a small bonus for their continued participation. The others would get the most intensive and personalized help that could be devised.

Worthwhile work

The two groups were matched as closely as possible in age, occupation, education and family. Those in ERA were assigned a specially trained adviser who would stay with them for nearly three years, available to meet at any time that suited them, in or out of the office, in a coffee bar round the corner or at 7 a.m. before work. The generosity of the offer was almost incredible. Clients could choose training up to a value of £1,000. Courses could be in a local college or with a private-sector trainer and in any subject accepted by the adviser as relevant to their life and work plan. Advisers also had discretionary funds on which participants could draw, if it would help them get or stay in work. The fund might pay for a mobile phone or for an MOT to keep a car on the road in order to get to work. It might cover the down-payment on a day nursery place: often two weeks has to be paid in advance. What astonished participants most were the cash incentives built into the scheme. Those who stayed in work for over thirty hours a week for thirteen weeks received a bonus of £400 to spend as they liked – and over the thirty-three-month period, they could draw up to six of these. In other words, just for staying in work they got a rolling bonus of £2,400, plus intermittent other money if they needed it.

Oddly, this element stopped some people agreeing to take part. They were convinced there must be a catch and they would have to pay it back sometime, which might lead them into debt. They were so used to phoney offers of money for nothing that they smelled a rat. Sometimes it was hard to get people to join the scheme at all, especially those who already had a job. Some of those in work who had no particular wish to move up, train or change job were simply perplexed at being offered cash just to keep going, obliged only meet their adviser regularly and listen to suggestions of what else they might do in life. Some people were indeed content to stay where they were, resolutely non-aspirational. They were happy in their jobs and could not be cajoled into aiming higher or seeking a better career.

Despite the existence of this unambitious group, overall ERA results have been excellent. ERA graduates did do better than on any other programmes. Compared with the control group, 7% more lone parents went into full-time work, as did 10% more of those who had been working part-time. Lone parents earned up to 29% more and 14% more chose to combine work with extra training, boding well for their future. Some 4% fewer ended up receiving any benefits or tax credits.

ERA cost £30 million, paying for well-trained intensive personal advisers, good-quality training courses, bonuses and cash to overcome crises. Extrapolate its results and over time the net benefits for society scale up, not just into large net savings for the public purse from extra tax revenues and reduced welfare cost but into an aggregate increase in well-being and productivity, with knock-on effects for these people's children. Here is another step towards social justice, measured by the lives and living standards of the poorest; another example of how a social investment by the state can help people move on up, and over time reap fiscal rewards. Only such intensive pro-grammes have any chance of realizing the target of moving 70% of lone parents into work by 2010.

We asked the ERA advisers what single change would help

get more people back to work. They spoke with one voice, and without hesitation: a higher minimum wage was their first and most urgent plea. The right to free school meals further up the earnings scale came next. The right to have a mortgage paid while in low-paid work: insanely, housing benefit pays rent but not mortgage once someone is in work, even on the lowest wage. Help with travel costs, which often tip the balance in making work not pay. More help with astronomical childcare costs, especially in London, which were the biggest barrier to work for single mothers. But above all, let there be some sort of intensive advisory scheme like the ERA pilot with good training paid for and available to everyone.

At the time of writing there is no plan to roll ERA out nationally. The upfront cost is high and there may be little political mileage in it. Of course the government should invest in it, but instead Labour ministers have preferred to make punitive threats to deny council housing to those out of work, and to make those looking for jobs do forced labour. It may play well with the tabloids, but it does nothing to tell voters what works – which is good schemes like ERA.

The ERA advisers' point about the minimum wage is critical. Redistribution can't just be about taxation: it can and should happen through the fairer repricing of labour and just rewards. The government itself is the direct or, via outsourced contracts, indirect provider of millions of low-pay service jobs, so the state can choose to pay whatever rate it likes. If it set its own basic pay well above the official minimum it would tug the jobs market upwards. The cost of public services would rise and so would taxes, but there would be savings to be made on tax credits – the more people earn in pay the less they need state support to top up their income to survive.

CHAPTER 10

Tomorrow's People

On a wet February morning in the Kentish Town health centre, Faruk Noor is meeting three of his regular clients. He is not a nurse or doctor in the conventional, clinical sense. Around the health centre, typical of modern London, the Victorian terraces are a middle-class haven, though just up the road is social housing, instantly recognizable as such. The borough of Camden owns 30,000 properties, housing some of the capital's less well-off citizens, yet middle-class homes know misfortune, which explains some of Noor's caseload.

He is a jobs doctor, a specialist adviser with a charity called Tomorrow's People. Its mission is to pick up those who have fallen out of employment and get them back into life and work. GPs in the centre refer cases: Kentish Town is a pioneer in locating a surgery and an advice centre together. In this practice of seventeen doctors enough of their 15,000 registered patients are depressed, off work and on incapacity benefit: unemployment itself has made many of them sick. Some don't work because of conditions such as backache and mild circulatory problems but they could if the right job were available and they were helped back on their feet.

A triumph of the modern era is that we are healthier and live longer. And yet many more people subsist on incapacity benefit (IB) than thirty years ago. Some 2.6 million working-age people are registered sick, drawing over £6 billion a year in benefits. Among them are those who can't work – the profoundly disabled, hopeless addicts, the seriously mentally ill, the sick and the dying. But hundreds of thousands of claimants are depressed, people who have been dumped in a benefit category and left to rot. Once out of work for six months, their chances of clambering back into employment get slimmer with every passing month.

The steep rise in IB claimants began in the dark days of mass unemployment. In the early 1990s the Tory employment secretary Michael Howard ordered civil servants to perform an administrative sleight of hand. Because invalids did not count as jobless, the trick was to put all the bad employment prospects on IB, so cutting unemployment totals at a stroke. Jobcentre Plus managers and GPs were happy to collude with ministers. Since jobs were impossible to find anyway, why not give the weakest and least likely prospects a bit of extra benefit by registering them as sick?

Now that official unemployment has fallen and jobs are plentiful, the fate of this forgotten mass has attracted the policy makers' attention. Labour moved to cut the number who become IB claimants by improving jobs advice for all who first claim benefits. But a backlog of claimants remains, half of whom say they would like to return to the world of work if only they had the confidence.

This underlines the conclusion of research that found work cured as well as caused illness.[1] Hence the Kentish Town programme, which has been a great success. Of 200 patients referred to an employment adviser, 55% went into training or voluntary work and 36% found a job. For this difficult group, that's a high hit rate. It's also a blessing for the doctors, relieving them of some of their most intractable patients. With twelve minutes for each consultation, how can GPs be expected to offer much help to people with hard-to-define physical and mental difficulties? The employment adviser has time. Patients are offered an hour of counselling, several times a week if necessary. What's more, he is on the end of the telephone to listen, encourage and support them. The programme has meant a 20% reduction in GP visits for these patients and a 19% reduction in antidepressant prescriptions.

Some of those Noor sees simply lost their footing and have found it immensely difficult to get back into regular employment. They are by no means all from poor or working-class backgrounds. Bad luck has never been confined to the lower orders. Although the odds are stacked heavily in favour of those born into secure middle-class homes, life chances offer no guarantee against an accidental slide down the social ladder. Here is another good reason why the comfortably off would do well to shorten the gap between top and bottom, so descents among their own kith and kin are not too vertiginous, with a cushion of social support to break their fall.

Just Rewards: The policies that work

On the Thursday morning we visited, it happened that all Noor's clients had once been doing well in life, high-flyers who fell out of the sky without a parachute. Even the self-assured on good incomes find that if they become detached from a career and don't find another opening soon, their entire world can implode. Disaster can happen more easily, more inexplicably and faster than we think. What happens when you've tried hard for a whole year to climb back up onto the ledge but no one answers your well-crafted job applications? Perhaps you are a little too old. Perhaps – catch-22 – because you aren't already in a job your application lacks credibility. Then the day comes when the Jobcentre tells you that your time is up. The moment has come to be 'realistic' about your chances and the pressure is on to take a job, any job, at the minimum wage if need be. It's made clear that there is a limit to how long the taxpayer can support your attempt to get back into a professional or managerial post. At that moment the abyss opens beneath your feet. Once in a manual job you may never climb out. What do you put on your CV now as you apply ever more desperately for a higher-grade post? How do you explain, how do you cover the shame? This low-level job will redefine who you are and where you belong in the pecking order. Once in work, with much less time, it will become difficult to go on searching for something better. In minimum-wage jobs you can't make personal calls and you can't go out to attend interviews. Flexibility in the hours you work is rare and job hunting becomes ever more difficult.

In this situation, you learn to take orders instead of give them. As you become the member of a lower caste of being, what do you tell friends and family? You think bitterly of the waste of that degree and all those years of education. Worse than all that, you are now about to lose your home because once you are in work your mortgage interest will not be covered by housing benefit. Housing benefit will cover even a high rent on a council or private flat, but not a mortgage. Falling down the social ladder can entail exit from home ownership.

The nightmare happened to Steve. A tall, confident-seeming man, with a relaxed air of authority, he had worked for nineteen years in retail, climbing the ladder to become a manager in the luxury-goods business. In his last job he was a top buyer with twenty-two other managers reporting to him. But the slight chill in the economy in 2005 hit the sensitive luxury sector. He found another job fast but it was less secure, so when he was finally made redundant again he could only get himself a short-term contract and then that came to an end. In his fast rise in a booming sector he had never contemplated failure. There always seemed to be plenty of other jobs if ever he wanted to make a move. Suddenly the music stopped and he had no chair. He was out of work for months at a time while retailers held back, sniffing the wind and waiting to see which way trade went before hiring. At forty years old, his age now seemed to make a difference. In no time at all blank months clocked up on his CV, workless months to be explained away. Steve was too experienced for certain jobs and all of a sudden his face didn't quite fit. He was completely and utterly unprepared to be this new person, a middle-aged man who couldn't get a job.

When the Jobcentre warned him that he'd have to take any

job, he stopped sleeping and went to his GP. Fortunately for Steve, Faruk Noor was at hand. 'Faruk asked if I was suffering from depression, but I said I wasn't – though I probably was. Who wouldn't be? He talked about confidence but I said I was fine. That was one thing I thought I certainly didn't lack. Yet I was empty inside, blank, I had lost everything.

'We had a very black session when I plunged right down into the depths. Bit by bit, Faruk has helped to build me back up. It took a lot of time, getting over the shock. But he persuaded me I could do it. I quit smoking, joined a gym, took up yoga which I used to think was rubbish. My jobseeker's allowance is £56 a week, which is hard, but now I'm back applying for jobs at £40k and get this – this morning I had my first real job offer. A job in Abu Dhabi that looks as if it might come off.'

Noor once had his own business and took to counselling as a volunteer. Now it has become his life's work. His clients all spoke of his skills with exceptional warmth, describing his patience, his way of gently edging them out of depression towards optimism. Advisers from the Tomorrow's People charity have no connection with the Department of Work and Pensions; government-employed advisers, brilliant though they often are, are obliged to balance their sympathy with the need to get Jobcentre clients off benefits and into jobs as fast as possible, to meet their target. Faruk need only act in his clients' best interests. He has no targets, yet he gets results.

Celia is a beautiful young woman who should be full of self-confidence. Instead she is painfully tentative and her eyes brim with impending tears whenever she speaks. 'I was in a high-powered, high-pressured media job,' she says. 'I was working very, very hard, a workaholic, night and day to tight deadlines until suddenly one day I lost it. Completely, altogether. I went to bed for months and never got up. I was porridge, I saw no one, I didn't speak, I did just nothing at all. I was so bad I didn't even know I was having a breakdown. I didn't know anything at all.'

Eventually a friend persuaded her to go the doctor, who gave her strong antidepressants. She wanted a course of cognitive behaviour therapy, but the waiting list was a shocking six months long – one of the worst NHS scandals, since it does such good to depressives. (In the 2007 comprehensive spending review, money was specifically allocated for cognitive therapy for those on invalidity benefit, so this should start to improve.) The GP referred her to Noor, where she had long sessions twice a week. 'I thought maybe a job would be a good idea, something small, quiet and easy. I'll never go back to a high-powered job. But Faruk says I'm not ready yet.' Indeed, she certainly doesn't seem ready for much, so raw and vulnerable still.

The third faller visiting Noor that day was Brian, a man of about fifty who had run his own family's furniture business all his life. As Ikea and the chains grew mighty they swept away the small independents and eventually his business failed. So here he was, a graduate and an accomplished businessman but inexperienced when it came to applying for work or indeed working for anyone else. With a child in secondary school, he had no way to earn a living. 'I don't think I would have got through this if my family hadn't been so very understanding. They haven't ever let me feel useless just because I haven't got a job.' But he did feel useless. It has been three years now since his company folded, but he says the counselling at the practice has helped. 'I never thought I lacked self-esteem, but having no job takes it away from you. Faruk is helping build it back.'

From time to time he bursts out in indignation at the state of the world – and in particular at the sheer bloody rudeness of employers who advertise jobs and don't bother even to acknowledge applications. How do they get away with it? How dare they not even have the courtesy to send a polite rejection? This wretched man comes from a middle-class world of equals where people answer letters and treat each other with a measure of civility. He is suffering the culture shock of living in that other ruthless world where the rest of the population live, where the boot is always on the employer's foot and would-be employees must genuflect, expecting to be rebuffed over and over again, until eventually finding favour. It should be illegal to advertise a job and never reply to applicants, he says.

Noor calms him down. 'Look, Brian,' he says, echoing Reinhold Niebuhr, 'you have to learn to concentrate on those things you can change and forget about those things you can't. Just work on the process of getting a job, step by step. Do what you can in the things that you can control.' Brian nods glumly but he always wants to rail at the state of world. Will he ever get a job? Noor thinks he will, and Brian feels better about himself after the counselling.

Individual circumstances are so various: no life trajectory can ever be determined in advance, which is why all social interventions will have a messy, even wasteful edge to them. But here is a scheme that appears to bring benefit, given the complicated problems of the people who end up unexpectedly unemployed for all kinds of reasons. Why not a Faruk Noor on hand in every surgery? Sited in a GP clinic, he is in the place where people feel safe and unthreatened, a medical haven that is not expected to judge or bully them. Faruk is a clever blend: he's a therapist for people who may not think they need therapy. He is a job adviser for people who may not think unemployment is the cause of their distress or that work might be a cure for their symptoms. He is independent, wishing the best for his clients; above all he gives them time, the most precious commodity in a rushed world.

He is all too rare. Tomorrow's People, founded some twenty years ago, has employment advisers in eighty GP surgeries but they would like to be able to offer advisers to the 500 other GP practices who are queuing up. They dream of making the service available in every practice. We lack a cut-and-dried evaluation of costs and benefits but the signs are that the NHS saves money. Each patient registered with the programme costs £720 on average but the service eases pressure on GPs and probably gets enough people back to work to more than pay for itself in savings to the benefits budget. It is a service which the state itself probably should not provide; it needs to be at arm's length. But it is one that government should pay for. Here is an example of how charity can innovate and the voluntary sector can provide an excellent service, but to make it available to all who might benefit, state financial support is vital.

PART FOUR

Just Rewards: Raising the money

CHAPTER 11

Philanthropy is no excuse

Your host this evening is Peregrine Banbury, who handles Coutts bank's landowning and prestigious clients. He is old money – a family tree with roots in the Norman conquest, ex-wife a Villiers – but happy to deal in new money too. He is MC-ing a charity event at the bank's Charing Cross offices, a splendid eighteenth-century exterior with its famous pepper-pot towers, the inside gutted and transformed into an airy atrium with plants and a pond filled with suitably fat goldfish. Coutts's other offices are in Jersey, Switzerland, the Isle of Man, the Caymans and Monaco – all tax havens. But as if to compensate for helping its clients avoid paying taxes Coutts is offering to help them give some money away wisely. Here is modern philanthropy in action.

Opening tonight's charity event, Banbury recalls the good works of Angela Burdett-Coutts, granddaughter of the bank's

founder. The nineteenth-century philanthropist, once reckoned the wealthiest woman in England, gave to a remarkable
array of causes, including drinking fountains, dogs, bees, an
archaeological survey of Jerusalem and primary schools. She
was a founder of what became the National Society for the
Prevention of Cruelty to Children. Hers is a neat illustration
of the randomness of charitable giving.

Banbury quotes Bob Hope: 'If you haven't got charity in
your heart, you've got heart trouble.' It is Coutts's belief, he
goes on, that 'a company that just makes money is a poor
company' and he sells his bank's advisory service on how to
make charitable donations tax efficient. Philanthropy has a
certain cachet these days, and some rich donors urge their
peers to give more. Sometimes it is mere ostentation, sometimes a collective instinct for self-preservation and sometimes
it is old-fashioned duty or guilt. Conversation soon turns to
the topic of donations and how to encourage more giving.
Chatting to the organizers and the regulars, they are keen to
encourage others to donate. What would get more of the
wealthy to give? 'Cut taxes' is always the first answer. 'If you
cut people's taxes, as they do in America, it would help. You
should give more tax breaks for charitable donors,' said one
regular participant at these events, and others strongly
agreed. What about paying higher taxes instead? 'Absolutely
not. That's just the state reaching into your pocket. That's not
giving,' said a man growing red-faced at the thought. A tall
and elegant woman in pearls said giving is an act of spontan-
eous generosity that binds people together. 'Forcing people to
pay is quite different in spirit!' Indeed it is. These were on the

whole generous-minded people who acknowledged that there was a problem with poverty, and philanthropy was to be their solution, hence the attempt to persuade others to give more.

The get-together at Coutts is sponsored by the Funding Network, which describes itself as 'a loose affiliation of individuals with a common purpose, to join in using our material prosperity to fund social change causes'. Around 200 regular givers belong to the network: they may give a few thousand on each of these evenings. Speed-dating for philanthropists, the event is intended to promote impulse-giving. First-timers get introduced to the charity habit and potential donors learn from serious givers. This is gentle stuff compared to City charity dinners, where big money can be raised in one evening amidst boasting and raillery.

At these Funding Network occasions, five small charities pitch for cash. They are to compete to attract money. After a welcome drink, we sit on little gold chairs while an auctioneer introduces them one by one. Their representatives have six minutes to make an impassioned plea before the strict time-keeper rings to cut them off. After the opening pitch they have another six minutes to answer questions.

Off they go! Number one is a small project in India offering training to young people whose fathers have been imprisoned for murder. No one will take these outcasts in. Their workshop lathes and skills are out of date and the Delhi government will give no more grants. The charity needs money to buy computers to teach the children modern skills. But the presentation on its behalf by a middle-aged British couple is faltering.

Number two starts with a case history describing an elderly rural postmistress in danger of losing her post office because of cuts in subsidies. The charity wants to give local people more say over what happens.

Next up is a businessman who founded a project in South Africa, using volunteers to teach 150 disabled children to read. Then the would-be donors hear of a scheme for volunteer retired accountants to offer tax advice to pensioners to minimize their tax payments: 'We find errors are almost always in favour of the taxman.'

Last is the charity that runs a world cup for homeless people, using football as a means of helping them to get their lives together. It is organized each year in collaboration with the *Big Issue* magazine and players from forty-eight nations are due to compete in the finals in Copenhagen.

Subjected to rigorous questioning, some stood their ground but other reps stumbled. When the giving started, donors called out their names, how much they were offering and which cause would benefit, while a running tally for each charity was flashed up on a giant screen. Regular benefactors stood ready to ensure none of the five lost and remedy any potentially embarrassing deficits in the giving stakes. In the end, learning to read in South Africa came top.

The charities each collected around £60,000 but they had been made to sing for their supper. There was a hint of the slave-market about the evening. 'Brother, can you spare a dime' isn't a song for the dignified. In the voluntary sector, fund-raising is the least welcome task; forms must be endlessly filled in to bag a grant from a foundation, numbers crunched to hit the target set by a government scheme, stage shows performed for a merry audience of the wealthy.

In recent years people with grand fortunes have started to add to their kudos by the manner of its disposal. Matthew 6:1 has few readers these days: 'Take heed that ye do not your alms before men, to be seen of them.' Philanthropy has become another way of exerting power and control. We attended a breakfast for high-net-worth individuals organized by the Charities Aid Foundation and hosted by the Lord Mayor of London at Mansion House. The main speaker was Stanley Fink, chief executive of Man Group plc, the hedge-fund managers. Charity, he made plain, was a way to fame and extra fortune. 'I want to talk about what charity can do for us,' he told them, describing giving as the ultimate door-opening lifestyle accessory. 'What do you do now you've got all the toys?' he asked. 'You've already got all the houses, yachts, cars and jets you can use, so what comes next is charity.' It's not just the joy of giving, but opportunities to meet celebrities: 'I get invited to places I'd never have seen otherwise.' Charity is the passport to the in-crowd: he listed the eye-popping names and places his philanthropy had taken him, from Number 10 upwards. Give and ye shall meet celebs.

At the behest of Labour ministers, the mega-wealthy such as Fink have taken to secondary education. In academy schools, for a very reasonable £2 million a pop, they get their name above the door plus the option to chair the trustees and, subject to governance rules, select like-minded members of the board. Sponsors thus play a major role in selecting and firing headteachers and designating specialisms, free of local authority control. 'If we can apply the entrepreneurial principles we have brought to business to charity, we have a shot at having a really strong impact, to be able to transform the lives of children,' says Arpad Busson, a Swiss-born financier, the founder of Absolute Return for Kids (ARK), which runs seven academy schools. This is a charity mentioned as often in the gossip columns as in *Society Guardian* because Busson helped turn giving into high fashion. ARK's 2007 fund-raising dinner is said to have raised over £26 million, exceeding the £18 million claimed in 2006, mainly on the back of pledges from Bloomberg, Merrill Lynch and UBS. Guests were entertained by Prince and items auctioned by the deputy chair of Sotheby's included a day on the set of the latest Bond movie and dinner with Mikhail Gorbachev. The previous year guests heard Elton John, and up for sale were a Damien Hirst and a guitar lesson from Chris Martin of Coldplay. Press releases name-check the producers, the food suppliers and the floral decoration: this is business as charity and vice versa.

Are the rich merely bidding to reclaim the position once occupied by aristocratic patrons, suzerains of the public sphere? They control the business sector so why not social policy as well? City entrepreneurs are used to running the show and think they know best, whether running schools, hospitals, universities, galleries or Jobcentres. The voluntary sector should be efficient and effective, of course, and corporate and finance-sector managers have a contribution to make. Financial skills are often in short supply and balance sheets and audit committees should truck no nonsense. But voluntary organizations are complex and attract diverse people. The business approach can be reductionist.

Why carp at charity? Think of the good causes being assisted. ARK money will help close orphanages in Bulgaria as well as sponsoring English inner-city schools. But many of the rich don't feel any responsibility outside their family; others don't have spare cash – they need every last penny of that £5-million-a-year income. In an Institute for Public Policy Research survey, Laura Edwards was told by one wealthy non-giver, 'I don't trust charities.' Some rich people said charities were too professional in their fund-raising and yet not business-like enough in spending money. She concluded that tax incentives and high-profile giving campaigns might encourage those already giving large amounts to up the ante, but the majority of wealthy individuals who give little or nothing are, she concluded, pretty impervious.[1]

When the Scottish sports-goods magnate Sir Tom Hunter announced he was giving away £1 billion over his lifetime, the story led the BBC *Ten O'Clock News*, perhaps underscoring how rare big giving is. Andrew Carnegie said a man who dies rich dies shamed, but it seems embarrassment is easily weathered. We explored attitudes in our focus group with highly paid City lawyers and bankers. They felt charities were not so different from government and would 'waste' money. One lawyer was candid. 'People like us don't put our hands in our pockets so much.' Another lawyer asserted, 'The general feeling is a lot of cynicism about whether or not if you do give the cash it's going to get where you want it to go.' Some have proposed allowing rich taxpayers to divert their money into charitable foundations, which would be under public supervision with the state allowed to nominate subjects for giving, though the processes would be outside government control. It would mean the rich could specify a donation to a foundation providing, say, bursaries for students from lower-income backgrounds to attend college. Our high earners were unimpressed.

It is true that the larger a household's annual income the more likely the household will give money to charity. Half the households in the top 10% of the income distribution make charitable donations but only one in six of the bottom 10%. But there is a twist in the figures. The parable of the widow's mite holds true still. The worse off give proportionately more of their income. The top fifth of households give less than 1% of their total income, while the poorest tenth give three times as much, or 3% of their income – not more absolutely, but more of the little they have. In relation to their populations, there are more donors in the poorer north-east of England than in the richer south-east. More women give than men, though women tend to have lower incomes.

Bluntly, the sheikhs at the front the camel train are a greedy bunch. Right-leaning think-tanks such as Civitas and Reform are simply wrong in their contention that charity could be propelled by rich givers into substituting for government (permitting taxes to be cut of course). They believe the welfare state killed the charitable impulse. Cut taxes and people will give more. Let us off capital gains tax and donations will swell. Yet the data do not bear this out. The best off don't donate even though charitable giving is already subsidized through income-tax concessions.

The Charities Aid Foundation notes that the same few names get recycled in the media, giving an erroneous impression that philanthropy is on the rise. Its own annual report for 2007 records 'a fall in the proportion of high-level donors' – and this in a year of soaring boardroom bonuses. As chancellor, Gordon Brown tried to bribe the rich with tax breaks. If the rich tire of one of their homes, they can now give it to charity and pay no capital gains tax. Ditto any shares they donate. Despite such incentives, the total value of giving in the UK remains steady as a proportion of total income at just 1% of GDP. What we have are near US-style tax rates without American-style charitable giving.

Charities are precious because they can innovate, tread new ground and test new solutions to social ills, but it is government that has to follow through and do the heavy lifting. The problem with philanthropy is not just its insufficiency. Consider that random list of causes supported by Angela Burdett-Coutts. Philanthropy is haphazard and scattergun. Most people, including those who say they want to give more, would prefer to give only occasionally, so giving just cannot be relied on to fund permanent social programmes on any great scale. In the academy schools the state pays the annual running costs. And donors can interfere, distorting priorities, demanding attention to pet projects. Camila Batmanghelidjh, charismatic founder of the charity Kids Company, has complained at the lack of expertise of the big-time donors who want to run her social programmes. A rare example of humility is Warren Buffet, the stock tipster and fund manager, who wants to direct his fortune not to a self-aggrandizing Buffet trust, but to existing projects paid for by Bill Gates.

Variety is the beauty and the limitation of charities. Diverse causes are registered, including animal welfare in Japan, Odin worship, donkey sanctuaries and a charity that spays stray cats. Admirable, but nothing to do with the transfer of well-being from the well off to the back of the camel train. Charity regulators can only make judgements about whether an applicant qualifies according to broad rules, then insist correct procedure is followed. They prevent fraud and misdirection of money, but they don't audit or rank charities for worthiness, effectiveness or efficiency. Nor can the Charity Commission and the Scottish regulator do much about advertising campaigns that often distort social issues, using images of child abuse to tug at heartstrings, for example, when the real cause is poverty. Charity chief executives are not subjected to rigorous external assessment, nor are their organizations. As long as they are not corrupt or flagrantly abusing their office, they can be personal empire builders. The press squawk when a charity chief is caught stuffing donations into her handbag, but rarely question charities' results in the way they tear apart government programmes. Millions sluice through the accounts of lifeboats and guide dogs virtually untracked; compare this to government spending, where every penny has to be accounted for and effectiveness is measured. Critics of taxation tend to choose the best of the private or the voluntary sectors to compare with the worst of the public sector, omitting the political and social complexity of public provision and its priorities.

Many charities are excellent. A self-confident and well-supported charitable sector underpins civil society, encourages pluralism and promotes the public provision of social services. The best charities combine business acumen and humane principles. Charity shops staffed by volunteers diversify homogenous high streets. A hospital volunteer's trolley is a warm non-institutional face in a world of medical hierarchy, while the care home run by a good charity can shape best practice for others. But charities cannot substitute for public provision, as they repeatedly say themselves. The reason that government services and spending grew as the UK industrialized in the nineteenth century is that charity failed miserably to provide adequate schools, social services or even churches. Utopians in right-wing think-tanks may advocate rolling back the state, and cuts in tax to Victorian levels, but it is nonsense to think that the voluntary spirit will kick in and charity will take care of the needy. The 'automatic presumption of public benefit from all types of charities appears open to challenge', according to a recent study, which showed that donating to art galleries, museums, universities and the like could exacerbate inequality, by benefiting the well off more than the poor. By donating and getting tax relief the sum available for redistributive taxation is cut, which makes philanthropy even more inegalitarian.[2] At that Mansion House breakfast we suggested to a major ARK donor that paying more tax might be a better way for the wealthy to pay their dues than random gift-giving. He answered that the state could never spend his money as well as he could. If he gives he can direct it exactly where he wants and oversee what happens to it. Follow this recipe to its natural conclusion and anarchy or plutocracy result. The rich are used to working in authoritarian company hierarchies where orders are given and obeyed. Government must work with the reasonable consent of the people, with checks and balances and strict accountability. That's what democracy is. At the heart of that donor's objection is a dislike of the core business of welfare states, redistributing income according to need and ensuring no one is left out because they lack money.

True philanthropy in the modern age is tax-friendliness: public acknowledgement that a reputable mechanism exists to extract money from those who have too much and give it to those who have nothing. Imagine the political impact if some of these wealthy philanthropists publicly praised the purpose of redistributive taxation. It would take only a small band of the City's clan chiefs to expose the unacceptable tax-averse culture of the rich. They could shame the non-domiciled, the private-equity tax evaders, the trust-fund inheritance-tax cheats and their attendant tribes of tax advisers bent on denying the state as much money as possible. By turning their fire on their own kind, they could raise far more money than they will ever be able to give away themselves.

They could do even more. Imagine if they themselves were to advocate a top tax rate of 50% on earnings over £100,000, affecting only the top 1.5% of the taxpaying population. This would bring in an additional £4.5 billion every year. If that extra tax were raised from the top earners and earmarked for the neediest, it would more than cover the £3.4 billion the

Philanthropy is no excuse

Institute for Fiscal Studies says is needed to lift half our poor children over the poverty threshold by 2010. That really is serious money. It is good to give – but it's even better to pay your taxes.

CHAPTER 12

Avoiding their fair share

Here was the pitch: Labour (hiss, sneer from the audience) has introduced fifty new taxes (gasp) but we can show you how to avoid them, all quite legally. Inheritance tax is a truck (cue PowerPoint slide of a *Duel*-style monster) barrelling down the highway to get you unless you take our advice.

In marbled Mayfair offices, the executive sales manager is describing a string of tax-avoidance schemes to an audience of late-middle-aged and elderly persons of property. Rarely has a seminar speaker commanded such rapt attention and ardent support from his listeners.

The invitation, printed on thick vellum, had offered a chance to attend an investment-strategy and inheritance-tax planning seminar, taking place at a firm called St James's Place. The event was held at its offices in Hamilton Place, an elegant side street tucked away from the traffic grinding round Hyde

186

Park Corner, boasting Wealth Management on its front door brass plate. This is a peculiarly blank part of London, full of transient foreign money, Rolls-Royce showrooms, faceless international boutiques and the businesses and the casinos of Curzon Street.

Watch out, the salesman counselled his avid audience. You may think you have successfully lodged a claim to be domiciled abroad, but remember what happened to Richard Burton. A tax exile, on his death he was buried in Wales, which gave the Inland Revenue a sneaky opportunity to declare him a UK resident, and his estate became liable for £2.4 million in inheritance tax. (Have they no mercy, no respect even for the dead?)

But you can, with our help, avoid paying inheritance tax. We clever analysts can stay one nimble step ahead of the grasping tax collectors by monitoring every twist and turn of Treasury policy. HM Revenue & Customs (HMRC) never officially approves any scheme and it keeps closing them down, but today's offering we know will work. (Eager curiosity.) Our top man, a QC, has checked it and he acts for HMRC itself in its own toughest tax-law cases. If HMRC were to change the rules, have no fear because regulations cannot be made retrospective. Here is how to give all your assets away for inheritance tax purposes and still spend what you like while you are alive. A client of ours just saved £3.5 million this way. (Sighs of admiration.) You can do this with a second property and all your other assets.

Then followed a diabolically complex scheme that involved setting up two trusts, with one trust lending money to the other.

187

On death, the first trust demands the money back from the second, and hey presto, the only money left in the second is £300,000, which happens to be the threshold for paying inheritance tax. Or something like that. Never mind the technical details. The point was: these clever, highly paid people work night and day to stay one jump ahead of far less well-paid HMRC staff.

Some may say it is the government's own fault for making the tax system too complicated. The CBI, alongside the Institute of Directors and the British Chambers of Commerce, like to protest at increasingly rococo tax laws, as the complex tax codes swell each year into fatter and fatter volumes. Oh for simplicity, they cry. The impenetrability of tax law has led to a bonanza for tax accountants in recent years, with starting salaries for the newly qualified jumping in the eighteenth months prior to 2007 from £37,000 to £47,000. But their protests about undue complexity are hypocritical.

Some of the added complexity comes from Gordon Brown and the propensity of previous chancellors for using tax incentives or tax penalties to change behaviour, adding to the fiddly details of what can be claimed and what must be paid. Companies investing in research and development get tax breaks and buy-to-let owners can claim mortgage interest against rental income. But much of the complexity is a direct result of loopholes devised by the likes of St James's Place, obliging HMRC to hunt them down and stamp them out with ever more regulations. Next time CBI business leaders accuse the chancellor of 'complexity', he should ask each of them politely to explain their own cat's-cradle avoidance schemes and offshore trusts: if they paid their fair share with no deviousness, he would simplify the tax codes.

The arch practitioner of flamboyant tax avoidance is Sir Philip Green, who despite running BHS, a company doing most of its business in British high street shops, is classified as a resident abroad, and spends a lot of time flying backwards and forwards to his home in Monaco. If that wasn't enough self-generated complexity, much of his fortune has been sequestered with his wife, not just – we have to assume – because he loves her dearly. If City panjandrums and the boardroom apologists at the CBI want simple and transparent, let's start with their own affairs, whereby not paying their social contribution has become almost a matter of principle.

The wealthy have nothing to complain about in Labour's treatment of their tax affairs. The Blair–Brown governments can be called generous, or possibly naive. One of Gordon Brown's first acts as prime minister was to set up a Business Council for Britain, including the king of private equity, Damon Buffini of Permira, and Sir Richard Branson. All were invited to a Chequers lunch to greet Alan Greenspan, former head of the Federal Reserve Bank, in September 2007 – the man who had failed to rein in the great low-interest credit boom that led to the sub-prime mortgage crash, and the global credit crunch. In the run-up to the March 2008 budget, the Business Council used its access to lobby the prime minister and the Treasury on taxes: its chair Mervyn Davies, chairman of Standard Chartered Bank, warned solemnly against doing anything 'rash'. He meant progressive (*Financial Times*, 3/3/08).

In opposition prior to 1997 Labour had fallen in love with

the idea of 'venture'. Sir Ronald Cohen, founder of Apax Partners, the private equity group, persuaded Gordon Brown in 2000 to cut the capital gains tax rate from the 40% inherited from the Conservatives to just 10%, to encourage start-up entrepreneurs. Cue talk about rugged, buccaneering enterprise. In fact it helped ignite an explosion in financial re-engineering, lubricating the flow of capital into fast-moving unaccountable funds – private equity – and stoking the predators' incentive to buy and sell companies and to dress up their resulting income as capital gains. Chancellor Nigel Lawson had aligned the rates of income tax and capital gains tax precisely to remove incentives to play around with what money was called.

A throwaway comment in a newspaper interview in June 2007 lit the blue touchpaper: 'Any commonsense person would say that a highly paid private equity executive paying less tax than a cleaning lady can't be right' (*Financial Times*, 3/6/07). Nick Ferguson, chairman of SVG Capital and private equity player, had, as the headlines said, broken the taboo. Partners were paid a base salary, on which they paid tax, but their earnings came from sharing in the profits of selling companies and these sums, assessed as capital gains, could sneak in under so-called taper relief, with the result that tax paid slipped to 10%. Brown, still in the waiting room at Number 10, promised action and in response the new chancellor Alistair Darling proposed to raise the capital gains rate to a flat 18% for all. The private equity barons protested loudly at this '80%' increase, up from a meagre 10%, but there was a pleased silence from all those owners of buy-to-lets, second homes, art and antiques, who suddenly found their capital gains rate fall from 40% to just

18%. It was a bonanza for many. As ever, the losers in any tax change make maximum noise, while the winners quietly pocket their gains with no public thanks.

The number of people who registered themselves as non-domiciled in the UK soared by 74% between 2002 and 2005 – reaching 130,000 by 2007. Anyone born abroad, or even anyone born here but with foreign parents, can slip through the loophole by registering as a non-domicile, even if they live in the UK permanently, always have and always will. It means they only have to pay tax on income brought into the country or earned here. That does not stop their accountants devising trusts through which income from abroad gets remitted. The UK has become especially appealing to Russian oligarchs, Indian steel barons and Greek shipping magnates, who enjoy life in London but prefer not to be taxed. The ultra-wealthy have flocked here to take advantage of a tax break with no parallel in other major economies.

Labour and especially Gordon Brown revelled in London's pre-eminence as a financial centre, without acknowledging that the cause was not some elixir of enterprise only drinkable by the Thames but favourable tax treatment of the super-wealthy. During the first decade of the new century, the UK seemed to be running a fire sale. Exiled Thai prime ministers and marginal baseball barons rubbed shoulders with pals of President Putin, buying football clubs, art and antiques, and Knightsbridge property on the corporate merry-go-round. Not much ended up as investment contributing to GDP growth. The rest of the EU looks on London's new status as the playground of the rich not with admiration but with a measure of disgust and anger at the opening of a tax haven where the global rich avoid paying their fair share in their countries or anywhere. Arguments in favour are put forward vigorously by companies that service the wealthy. Patrick Stevens, tax partner at Ernst & Young, says 'all of these people bring huge amounts of economic activity and wealth to the UK'. That may be true but the question is about 'deadweight' – wouldn't they have come to London anyway, so the tax bait is unnecessary? Football clubs are not for sale in the Bundesliga or the top of Serie A, and some might say there is only one Chelsea.

There are profound issues of principle at stake here, too. The Blair–Brown government's message to the global mega-wealthy was: welcome to London. Enjoy the privilege of living in a safe city with a thousand and one amenities and, by the way, they are all paid for by the little people, not by you. The roads are free, police and security is free, the education of your staff is free, while the fire service will cut you out of your Porsche if it crashes and ambulances will pick you up and put you back together. Never mind the resentment you cause to those who do pay tax. Martin Wolf, economic commentator of the *Financial Times*, argues 'if we take the principle that successful people are too important and too mobile to pay tax to its logical conclusion, political community will collapse'. Footloose plutocrats shuttle between Monaco and Mumbai and, in Robert Peston's words in *Who Runs Britain?* (2008), within a decade 'public services would be creaking for lack of resources as the burden of tax fell on dwindling numbers of private-sector employees'. The real disposable incomes of the majority would be squeezed, power would shift to the rich and 'elected politicians would seem less and less relevant to the daily lives of the majority'. What sort of model are the non-doms for the rest of the tax-paying population, if not cheerleaders for avoidance and evasion? Martin Wolf asserts that a basic principle for the UK is 'to tax the world-wide incomes of all long-stay residents on the basis of ability to pay . . . If application of that great principle means some rich people leave the country, so be it' (*Financial Times*, 7/3/08).

In autumn 2007 the Tories seized the initiative on non-doms. Right from their first year of residence, non-doms should pay a flat tax of £25,000 a year on their non-UK income. It was a start, certainly enough to scare Labour into stealing the idea and suggesting £30,000 – but only after non-doms had lived in the UK tax-free for seven years. The Liberal Democrat shadow chancellor Vince Cable came closest to the principle of tax uniformity, arguing non-doms should declare their worldwide income to HMRC after seven years' residence, and pay tax on it. The parties play shuttlecock, with Labour constantly looking over its shoulder at the City and business lobbies. In February 2008 the Lord Mayor of London rudely chided the secretary of state for business at a City dinner, saying Labour's modest move 'threatens the prosperity of the whole country'. The vehemence of the non-doms' reaction and their threats to decamp in the face of a paltry £30,000 payment was at first puzzling. Why the fuss over peanuts? But behind the headlines the real row was over the small print where Labour was proposing that non-doms reveal their foreign possessions and earnings. Many had secrets they wanted none to know. More than that, Labour was planning to shut down the most lucrative aspects of non-dom status – their freedom to buy and sell British property and assets in the name of offshore trusts, owing no UK tax on capital gains and allowing them to compete in the property market on unfair terms. When the details were published in the March 2008 budget it looked as if Labour had stuck to its guns: the headline proclaimed the non-doms would indeed pay their £30,000 a year. But the small print showed the Treasury had quietly dropped the non-doms' crucial offshore trust capital gains bonanza. Their muted protests were understandably only formulaic, but enough to make Labour promise never to look again at their tax status, not for all of this or the next parliament. But at least, and at last, the status of non-doms has entered the political arena.

Contemplating the finance acts passed since 1997 you could not accuse Labour of inaction. But, as with capital gains, the Blair–Brown governments combined a certain naivety with a boy-scoutish enthusiasm for the good things that tax generosity ought to secure from business, such as more enterprise or more investment. Writing just as New Labour came to power, Richard Whiting noted in *The Labour Party and Taxation* (2000) how, during the twentieth century, the party had thought, in Pollyanna style, that we all basically believe progressive tax is a good thing and everyone should contribute according to their means. The Tories more or less agreed in principle if not in day-to-day practice, at least until Margaret Thatcher came to power, though even she increased the overall tax take by 3% during her reign. One consequence, so Whiting argues, had been laziness on the part of Labour policy makers, who never made the effort to understand the lengths that taxpayers, especially those on higher rates, will go to to avoid payment. Labour had ceased to make the moral case for tax as a contribution to community, a buoyant expression of the possibilities of living together in society.

His criticism continues to apply. As chancellor, Gordon Brown chose stealth and failed to make the political case for the public good of taxation. It is more by fortunate accident than by design that the UK retains an admirable professional cadre of tax gatherers who derive job satisfaction and stimulus from their own moral code of just and proper social contribution, without relying on communitarian speeches by ministers.

The financial advisers we visited in Mayfair are a mainstream firm, founded by some respected names: Jacob Rothschild, Denis Stevenson, Mark Weinberg, all of them knighted or elevated to the peerage. Does St James's Place contribute to growing GDP, the creation of employment or exportable entrepreneurial innovation? Hardly. Right-wing economists try to plot a line between marginal reductions in tax with rising enterprise and growth, but they can't pretend that crafty manoeuvrings by nifty tax advisers adds to the national wealth: Sir Philip Green's booty trickles down Monaco's Rue Grimaldi, where you won't find many British Home Stores customers.

But St James's Place is under surveillance. Most citizens pay as they earn, their taxes deducted at source with no chance to defraud the public purse even if they wanted to. Collecting their tax is routine HMRC work. But there is an elite group of inspectors waging perpetual battle against the tax advisory outfits. Tax headquarters are now at 100 Parliament Street, the Edwardian pile at the foot of Whitehall. HMRC is not just a world of process, rulebooks and calculation, but also, as it should be, a place of firm moral judgement.

Greed, greed, greed. It's a word used all the time by one senior inspector of taxes who has spent his career chasing people who seek to defraud the state by concealing their property and refusing to pay their share. He can't go on the record, but don't imagine some hatchet-faced bureaucrat limping feebly after the wily tax advisers. He is as sharp as a knife and disarmingly funny. In line with Whitehall's preference for bright people from non-specialist backgrounds, his degree was in classics. When he strides into company boardrooms, armed with details of their close-to-the-wind dealings, he not only can read them the riot act over their fiscal obligations but also, quoting Cicero, can lecture them on their civic duty.

His civil service pay in 2006 was £155,000, which includes a small bonus. Puzzlingly, the House of Commons Treasury committee had a go at HMRC bonuses in a report in March 2008, as if incentives were either unnecessary or extravagant – the MPs should try telling that to our man's customers. He could command many multiples of his salary as a private client adviser and time was when the Inland Revenue, as it used to be called, worried about the talent it was losing. Not now, or at least rarely, he says. As it happens, a middle-level member of his team was about to go to a merchant bank for a salary of £250,000 but 'they usually come back', he says. Why? 'They miss the intellectual challenge here. They miss the team and they miss the public ethos. In the end, enjoyment of the job matters to them more than the money. I love my job. I love public service.'

Our inspector produces the most cogent rebuttal of those who claim cutting tax would be good for the economy and that a simpler tax system would reduce evasion. He recalls budget day in 1986 when the Tory chancellor Nigel Lawson announced that the top rate of income tax was being slashed to 40% in a budget speech that had to be suspended in the Commons due to the uproar it caused. Inspectors thought they had had it. 'We were almost in tears. We thought we'd soon be out of a job.'

Conventional economic wisdom was that tax cuts would remove the incentive to cheat. 'We thought that once tax was so low, they'd all pay up, no problem. There would be no more need to bother with tax fraud or evading.' As Lawson asked at the time, why would well-off people bother to cheat now they could keep most of their money with tax payments so much smaller? Right-wing think-tanks believe that if you chop the rate of tax even lower, it actually brings in more revenue. The theory is that people are motivated to pay and you save on the salaries of tax clerks and inspectors. At a stroke tax advisers become redundant and offshore havens disappear. Except it didn't happen. After Lawson's budget, to the Inland Revenue's surprise, tax avoidance blossomed along with evasion and other frauds. Greed triumphed. 'When people had more, they seemed to want to keep even more of it. It changed the atmosphere in some important way. It tipped a balance,' says our tax inspector. Lawson spawned the loadsamoney late-1980s culture where it became more not less acceptable to brag about cheating the taxman. The Thatcher government, in stating its public disapproval of taxation, helped fashion a general anti-tax mood. Our tax collector recalls the birth of scams great and small, the new ways people found to hide their money from Inland Revenue scrutiny. Some were merely ridiculous, like paying large sums into a credit card account; the money earned no interest but was thought to be safe from the inspectors' eyes. One man, some years back, was found to have bought millions of Green Shield stamps as a way of hiding cash.

Recently companies have invented exotic methods to conceal payments and avoid tax. One involved paying employees in apparently low-value shares in Bahamas-based companies on which they pay a limited amount of tax. A decade later the shares miraculously rise in value, just when the owner decides to live in the Caribbean for long enough to avoid UK tax, and collect winnings worth millions. City bonuses have been concealed, given in certificates of ownership in things which decline in value. If you can delay the payment of tax you obviously pay much less.

Scams can be done with hay, cheese and tea – even in Turkish money. One finance house paid bonuses in Turkish lira, which until 2004, when it was revalued, was a sure-fire bet for depreciation. The employee was given a 'loan' worth, say, £1 million for a two-year duration, to be paid back in lira. The employee promptly transferred the sum into sterling. When the money had to be paid back, the lira was worth a lot less and the employee pocketed the difference tax-free.

HMRC is not without resources or imagination. The war on scams is never ending and close fought. A recent obligation on banks to disclose clients' foreign bank accounts will help: our inspector reckons that fewer than half of such accounts are honestly disclosed in tax returns. Incidentally, he keeps a sharp eye on St James's Place, sending his spies into their presentations and to other similar firms.

Designers of tax-avoidance schemes now have to register them with HMRC and each plan is given a number which taxpayers must mark on their returns, which sounds an alarm bell with inspectors. 'We give them this warning. Any tax return carrying one of those registration numbers we regard as very risky. It alerts us and we will scrutinize it with special interest. So bit by bit we are curbing the tax-planning industry. Be warned.'

Members of our senior inspector's team are required to bring in at least three times their salary: on average they do far better and that multiple can go up to 500 times. Why not employ many more of them, boosting the tax take further? The Department of Work and Pensions puts out a self-congratulatory press release when it employs extra staff to inspect benefit claims; but HMRC treads on eggshells in matters of staff numbers. Inequality in wealth is mirrored by inequality in the way fraud and evasion are handled. Consider the shock and awe directed at the criminal poor and the political silence about tax fraud. Imagine ministers naming and shaming tax evaders as they do estate youths committing anti-social acts. In comparison, the Republic of Ireland does have a policy of publicly identifying tax cheats. Every quarter the names of offenders are printed, making front-page news. Recently the head of the Irish public accounts committee was shamed this way. Finland,

Norway and Sweden require tax returns to be publicly available in the same way that wills are published. Why not in the UK? Are social obligations really a private matter? Public tax returns would allow high earners to boast of their tax contributions. Tax fraud would be cut with greater transparency – friends and neighbours might get suspicious at undeclared income. 'It would help a lot,' says our tax man with great regret, 'but can you imagine any British politician daring to suggest it? If I sent that up to the Treasury as a serious proposal they'd have the screaming abdabs.'

Yet, after the first electric shock of disclosure, things would soon settle down. We have transparency for the salaries of public officials, so why not for the incomes and public tax obligations of citizens at large? Transparency is a good tool against unjust inequalities, as employers often rely on staff keeping silent about what they earn, through shame or fear. Publishing pay on the office notice board would ensure that no one – women especially – is unfairly disadvantaged. Secrecy in tax and income matters begets injustice, harbours fraud and creates an atmosphere of paranoid unease about status.

Sometimes conscience does seize people who have been defrauding the state for years. Each year an amount of guilt money is paid anonymously, and a surprising number contact HMRC to confess to cheating; usually they are elderly and don't want to leave tax-fraud chaos for families to cope with, so a deal is struck. It's the British way, to take the money rather than to make an exhibition of people. As for the non-doms and the global mega-wealthy who have come to London, inspectors make fine judgements about residency, who qualifies and who over-steps their licence. Tax collection is something the UK traditionally does well in comparison with other countries and, along with the Netherlands, the cost of compliance with UK tax law is among the lowest in the league tables. But even in a country with one of the lowest top income-tax rates in the thirty industrialized OECD countries, it still seems that the better off people are, the harder they try to avoid paying their fair share. The more people have, the more they want to get away with.

Our inspector would like to boast that HMRC is bringing in more each year due to his colleagues' detective skills. 'But I can't claim that. Yes, we are getting better, but not that much better. Evasion is getting more prevalent and I'm afraid that is why we are detecting more of it every year. There is more of it, and the average amount we find in each case is rising.'

The inspectors work within political reality with admirable *esprit de corps*. 'The cleverest people I know work in this office,' boasts our man, and that's a comforting thought. Temptation exists, as bribes, presents and holidays are dangled, but the UK tax inspectorate is remarkably clean. Machines are used to do routine checking and the brains are reserved for dogged pursuit. 'We'll say to the small-fry cheaters, we'll leave you alone for four years but if we find you have been backsliding when we next check, you're dead. And it works, mostly. You can often frighten people out of playing endless ducks and drakes with us.' When it comes to the big fish, he says he can make deals. Come clean, pay the back tax, the interest and a 10% fine and that's the end of the matter – though some suggest a more punitive approach is in order. Such pragmatic willingness to strike deals with the super-rich misses a chance to name what is, make no mistake, theft. They steal, not just from the state but from fellow citizens on lower incomes, and double the effects of their avoidance and evasion by reducing the government's capacity to improve the life chances and earnings potential of the worst off.

CHAPTER 13

What needs to be done

Businesses and individuals can switch their capital between countries by moving their location, and they use it as a perpetual threat. But the impact of globalization on national governments has been exaggerated, as Lord Sainsbury concluded recently after reviewing evidence for the Treasury: 'Countries have not lost their ability to regulate and tax their economies, as the highly taxed but internationally competitive Nordic countries demonstrate. Quality outputs commanding high prices can only be made with quality inputs: skilled labour, a productive science base and an attractive business environment. Taxes well spent will boost an economy's productivity.'[1]

Reaction to the financial meltdown of 2007 showed central banks and finance ministries in North America, Europe and the Far East could still intervene, adjust, and regulate in their

national interests. The impact of globalization on social programmes has been talked up, but welfare states have not
imploded and countries still make their own exceedingly
diverse decisions about redistribution.[2]

As for the UK, it doesn't need a revolution to tax more fairly
and to spend the proceeds on social improvement: the distance
travelled (at least in rhetoric) by the Tories under David
Cameron illustrates the way the political landscape has shifted,
opening the argument both about excess at the top and inade-
quacy at the bottom. It would take relatively modest shifts in
policy to reverse the 'nothing can be done' fatalism of the last
decades, a fatalism often condoned by Labour ministers in
what they say, rather than what they have done. Sure Start,
Every Child a Reader and activist employment schemes
demonstrably make a huge difference to life chances and we
need to put more public money into them and similar initiatives. In the long run more social investment will generate more
tax revenue, as Labour found when its New Deal began to cut
the costs of unemployment and reap the rewards of 2 million
more people working and paying tax. To promote that virtu-
ous circle may not need more taxation in total, but new
contours for who pays what. We believe that tax reform at the
top, coupled with renewed intervention at the bottom, would
make all the difference to inequality in Britain today. Below we
have laid out a series of reforms which will set Britain on the
path to fairer rewards.

It's time to create a pro-tax and or anti-avoidance culture. The
general case for tax is rarely made. We are stuck in a groove

etched by the wealth-possessors and their political representatives; they propagate the message that taxation is negative, a
burden which demotivates workers. Refutation starts with
basic information. The last chairman of the Board of Inland
Revenue, before it merged to become HMRC, Sir Nick
Montagu, proposed sending out explanatory papers and pie
charts with assessment forms giving taxpayers basic information about where their money was spent. The government
could try to educate and explain, for example, that income
tax provides only a proportion of tax revenues (under a half
even if National Insurance is counted with it) while reminding
middle- and upper-class taxpayers just how much they benefit
from public expenditure – not just on the big-ticket items such
as health and defence but on social programmes that improve
both the well-being and economic potential of their fellow citizens. For the purposes of greater equality, leave for another
day the second-order debate about how best the state should
deliver each service – nationally, locally, through state, voluntary or private contracts. Unless strong voices keep saying that
public well-being depends on a redistributive government, the
nihilists and privateers gain ground. They will never be short of
useful negative anecdotes and bad examples that 'prove' nothing works and taxes are always wasted.

The work of arm's-length bodies such as the Institute for Fiscal
Studies could be expanded. This non-profit, independent body is
admired and trusted for the quality of its reports into tax and
spending and it is sponsoring a large inquiry into UK tax, led by
the Nobel laureate Sir James Mirrlees. Due to report in 2008, it
will help dispel prevalent myths about excessive 'burdens'.

Action by government does not need to start with tax rates or even the distribution of taxes and benefits: just collect more of the existing taxes that are due, stand up to the avoiders and their lobbyists, expose their claims that the sky will fall if loopholes are closed. A good maxim in tax is: let the light shine in. Make what we owe and what we pay transparent, so everyone can see who is living on means far beyond the income on which they have paid tax.

Let's start at the top. Just as there is a Low Pay Commission to settle the annual rate of the minimum wage, it is time to apply the same thinking to remuneration at the top. A High Pay Commission should be set up, not to set a statutory top rate, but to draft an indicative maximum, a reference figure. The Liberal Democrats have explored setting a benchmark after assessing business conditions and corporate performance. The commission would ask if profits or share price movement was so exceptional that huge increases in boardroom pay were justified each year. The High Pay Commission could inform the debate about any hard-to-justify pay packages. Non-executives and remuneration committees could use its findings to repulse the self-interested recommendations of the pay consultants; if it did not stiffen directors' sense of reason and decency at least it would make them more aware of the norm, and open them to public criticism if they flouted those norms. The commission might also demand to know why a company could close an occupational pension scheme at the same time as paying its directors pensions worth hundreds of thousands a year. It would cry 'windfall' when it saw unreasonable winnings pour into boardroom pockets. Naming and shaming can hurt.

What needs to be done

By subjecting a company's annual results to cool appraisal – of a kind that the market does not supply – the commission could judge pay rates in the light of longer-run trends and the national mood.

The days are long gone when governments tried to fix pay and prices. Pay policy was an act of desperation by both Labour and Conservative governments of the 1970s in a time of oil-shocked inflation: even Mrs Thatcher had a pay policy in her 1979 manifesto. To get round the policy, pay norms were broken by top earners who found devious ways to reward themselves in perks. But pay policy wasn't altogether a failure either. Those perks were tiny compared to the bonuses awarded now: not even a company Ferrari would match the bonus money awash in boardrooms today. The unions occasionally broke legal pay norms – and yet these national benchmarks did set a general level against which people could assess the fairness of their own wages.

If the state can tell NHS, school and council staff that their pay increases must stay within and below the inflation rate, how can the government pretend to have no view about a 37% average pay rise in the boardrooms of FTSE companies in a single year, with no demonstrable connection to corporate performance? Nervous politicians should note that addressing excessive pay would be popular: a *Financial Times*/Harris Poll found 60% of the public thought the government should go further, and actually cap the earnings of senior executives (*Financial Times*, 22/7/07).

Changing the culture of uncontrolled reward might be easier than the politicians think, as the mood is turning already. When blame for the 2007–8 credit crunch was laid firmly at the door of reckless bankers, the spotlight shone on their exorbitant bonuses as part of the cause, since they were paid for doing whatever it took to inflate short-term share price, regardless of the risks they took. None of the risks were to their own pockets. In March 2008 the Institute of International Finance, the association of global banks, met in Rio de Janeiro and for the first time discussed a voluntary code of conduct on bankers' pay. Ideas at the meeting included deferral of bonuses until the impact of a strategy was clear, or even clawing back bonuses in the light of later worse performance. Shareholders, pension funds and taxpayers have a stake in these bonuses, since they end by bailing out the banks. A *Financial Times* leader (8/3/08) warned, 'Bankers do have to understand that if they do not act to curb the worst excesses themselves, regulators are likely to be under fierce pressure to do something instead'. A High Pay Commission would assist self-regulation.

Journalists could help their fellow citizens think anew – by paying sharper and regular attention to how companies reward performance, for example. We glibly buttonhole ministers in the House of Commons and demand accountability; most details of their lives and pay are transparent and on the public record. But companies are fortresses and journalists tend to quail at the ramparts. Mysterious tycoons appear in the gossip columns, not the business pages, and the webs of brokers and City networks go largely under-reported.

Once earnings are outed, fairness can be assessed. The Association of Chartered Certified Accountants (ACCA), not a body of radical insurgents, asks for companies' annual reports to include a standard measure to track board pay relative to what employees get. It recommends that companies should declare publicly what they pay their chief executives as a multiple of average employee earnings.

It's time to make the honours system honourable. Here is an easy gesture that would signal the end of the culture of tax avoidance, but politicians often seem to have forgotten the power of symbols. The honours system tells us who are valuable and reputable members of society, yet knighthoods and other gongs are handed out regardless of how much effort the recipients have made to avoid paying fair taxes. The government could tomorrow instruct the honours scrutiny committees to adopt a new criterion: cross-check every recommendation for honours with HMRC records. Non-payers and ostentatious avoiders don't get membership of the Order of the British Empire or any other medal. Perhaps an enterprising historian could be given access to correlate past business and entrepreneurial honours with tax-avoidance activity. Until their tax regime is settled, people who live here under the non-domicile rule for tax should simply not qualify for honours, regardless of how much they have given to the National Gallery or the Royal Opera House. The arts make formidable lobbyists but the director of the Tate knows full well that the taxpayers (and to a lesser extent those who purchase lottery tickets) support the great majority of his shows, including the fabric of his gallery. Maximizing tax returns in the long run is in the interest of the arts, as of every other activity supported by the state. The core principle says that honoured citizens behave honourably – and tax avoidance is dishonourable. The whole scheme of gongs would be raised in public esteem if such tests were applied.

Membership of the House of Lords, where British laws are made, should only be for those who pay British taxes. The Liberal Democrats propose to remove anyone non-domiciled from the Lords, to ensure law-makers obey the same tax rules. They could go further and rule that any peer with an elaborate tax-avoidance scheme and offshore accounts also forfeit their seat.

Closing tax-avoidance loopholes could raise more than increasing tax rates. Lobbyists try a sleight of hand, claiming that full implementation of existing tax demands would be tantamount to a tax increase, and would frighten the wealthy away. They are trying to protect the enormous sums due to government if everyone actually paid the headline rates Parliament has set. Collecting what is owed could simultaneously permit more spending – on children, for example – and cuts in the rate of income tax and/or increases in personal allowances. A report for the TUC by Richard Murphy estimated that the Treasury fails to receive £25 billion a year because of avoidance by companies and wealthy individuals.[3] Companies whose payment of tax is completely incommensurable with the size of their business in the UK include BSkyB, Hanson, Legal & General and British Land plc. Some companies manage, within the law, to reduce their corporation tax obligations by buying and selling through wholly owned companies located in tax havens – including the Guardian Media Group. But is it corporate social responsibility to seek to minimize your contribution to the common pool of revenue? Through avoidance schemes big companies pay on average two thirds of the 30% official rate of corporation tax. Their spokespeople claim they would be failing in their duty to shareholders if they didn't seek tax loopholes, but what about failing in their duty to customers who are taxpaying citizens? By starting to challenge companies more vigorously over their capital allowances and their trick of loading up on debt in the UK, in order to offset their interest costs against profit, the HMRC raised an extra £2.7 billion in the four years prior to 2007 (*Financial Times*, 28/8/07).

Minimizing the 'tax gap'. In the 2008 budget, HMRC for the first time published its estimate of the difference between taxes owed and taxes paid. Hedged around with all sorts of qualifications because the boundary between legal avoidance and illegal evasion keeps shifting, the gap was estimated for 2005 at between £11 billion and £41 billion. Individuals owe up to £23 billion at 2005 prices, while companies are £13 billion short on corporation tax; the remainder is a shortfall on inheritance tax and stamp duty. The HMRC is tentative, reckoning the tax gap could be as high as 15% of liabilities. The Americans confess to a figure of 14% and the Swedes, who take tax collection very seriously, estimate they are 10% short. Behind these figures is a human reality: rich people acquire a fascinating fiscal invisibility. The admired entrepreneur Stelios Haji-Ioannou of EasyJet, who received a knighthood in 2006, says, 'I have no UK income to be taxed in the UK,' which is little short of a financial wonder.

Tax havens have been tolerated for far too long, protected by the powerful interests that use them. The German tax authorities learnt in 2008 of the scale of evasion practised courtesy of Liechtenstein's secretive banks. Other countries found their nationals too had hidden money in bank vaults in the tinpot principality. Other Alpine states, Switzerland and Austria, along with Andorra and Monaco, are under renewed pressure from the OECD to cooperate with finance ministries in other countries. President Nicolas Sarkozy should consider emulating his hero, Charles De Gaulle, who in 1962 stationed the French army around Monaco's borders, by way of persuading the statelet to share fiscal data.

The US Internal Revenue Service reckons its losses to tax havens at $100 billion. When the White House was stirred to action after 9/11 in pursuit of hidden terror accounts, George Bush threatened to sever the interbank service from the Bahamas, and it capitulated at once. But since then Washington's ardour has been doused by Wall Street lobbyists. Havens do not just conceal tax payments, they harbour the proceeds of bribery, drugs and dictators' stolen fortunes, and they pay for terrorism.

The UK is associated with tax havens of varying degrees of respectability. The Isle of Man, Jersey and Guernsey are crown dependencies. The UK Parliament could easily force them into full transparency, obliging them to declare who has bank accounts there. Successive UK administrations have winked as these islands established themselves as platforms for avoiding tax; they enjoy UK protection, commercial access and citizenship, yet conspire to reduce the UK tax take. It's time the fiscal anomaly ended. The overseas territories, specifically Anguilla, the British Virgin Islands and the Caymans, may be delightful relics of the colonial past, but why should banks located there be permitted to hide information from the UK tax authorities?

What needs to be done

The UK government should stop seeking to win the plaudits
of the City by soft pedalling on initiatives to improve the flow
of data on tax avoidance between countries. The UK single-
handedly maimed a 2005 savings directive from the EU which
demanded more information and called for taxation of income
from tax havens. Brown, as chancellor, insisted that the tax
authorities did not need to be told when cash was transferred
to offshore trusts or companies, prompting a rash of spurious
corporate registrations. The UK should stop holding out
against an EU plan to harmonize the way taxes are levied,
which would prevent any exploitation of loopholes between
countries – a proposal with no bearing on how each country
decides what to tax and at what rate.

*Numbers registering as non-domiciles have shot up in recent
years, forcing political parties to promise action.* The New
Testament said 'render unto Caesar that which is Caesar's',
not 'allow him only the pennies a clever tax lawyer will let you
get away with'. It certainly didn't say avoid rendering anything by pretending you don't really live in Jerusalem and are
merely a sojourning Egyptian. The principle is simple: long-
term residents of the UK pay UK taxes on all their income. It
cannot be so radical if it's the same principle applied by successive
American administrations, Republican and Democrat. Live in
the UK, pay UK tax. It doesn't take chapters of statute law
to spell out what living here long-term entails. If, as a consequence, a few Russian larcenists depart, well and good. Brian
Barry, in *Why Social Justice Matters* (2005), crisply observed
that an exodus would be something to welcome, since it would
reduce inequality in the UK at a stroke. The truth is, debate

213

over non-doms is an evidence-free zone. Threats of departure are bandied about, but no one quite knows where they would go, just as the claimed trickle-down benefits of having rich non-doms living in London are rarely quantified. Possibly no key players would depart. Those few who preferred living on rocky islands or Alpine wastes to the joys of London would be welcome to count their millions elsewhere.

Non-doms have accumulated many privileges, some of their tax exemptions unknown in other OECD countries. It's time they paid capital gains tax on properties they buy and sell in the UK. Non-doms may not choose to belong to the taxpaying community of UK citizens, even if they have lived here all their lives, but these 130,000 people do appear to wish to play a remarkable part in our political life. They buy the ear of power. A tenth of the money raised by political parties in 2001–7 – as declared to the Electoral Commission – came from non-dom sources; Labour, the incumbent party, was the principal beneficiary (*Observer Business*, 7/10/07). The remedy for this act of interference is simple: proscribe their donations to parties, cap all individual donations and move to a rational regime of party funding, paid for easily enough out of the enhanced tax take from abolishing their privileges.

Tax transparency is the best guarantee of honesty. If wills are made public, why shouldn't tax returns be public once they are posted? Whistleblowing is a decent pursuit, and if we could see what our neighbours are declaring as income, it would be a civic duty to report any obvious discrepancies with the way they are living and spending. If that provokes a squeamish reaction, it only goes to show how deep the anti-tax sentiment runs and how shallow is the notion that paying money to government is a noble, even a precious thing. Tax cheats should be treated in the same way as benefit cheats. Posters in the City or pop-ups on business websites should urge business people to shop one another to a tax-cheat helpline, the way posters and bus-stop signs in poor areas urge people to shop benefit cheats.

Moral climates have to be created. Our tax inspector said his political masters would have 'the screaming abdabs' if he were to suggest anything so radical as public tax returns. But companies make their tax declarations public and markets continue to operate – often more effectively because of extra information. Tax liabilities are a public matter and they could even be a source of pride. The salaries of public officials are public information and company reports allow access to aggregate figures for boardroom pay, at least in plcs, though it can be hard to decipher individuals' packages.

Coyness, secrecy and chicanery would disappear if taxable earnings went on the record. After the initial shock two things might happen. Power would shift from employers who could no longer play staff off against one another, and performance might improve, as pay and output became publicly linked. Transparency is a necessary condition for greater equality, and it would certainly narrow the gender pay-gap if women could make a quick comparison with the pay of the men sitting at adjacent desks.

Capital gains tax needs to be reconnected with the real world. The aim is to restore the lost equilibrium in taxation, to remove perverse incentives to reclassify or rechannel income for tax purposes. That means setting the same tax rate for income and capital gains with no greater divergence for corporation tax. The lesson of Labour's runaway decade has been that politicians listened too naively to pleas to make the UK a good place to do business, which led to Labour cutting both CGT and corporation tax, opening the door to taxing the wealthy less than before. One perverse effect of bringing all CGT down to just 18% has been to reduce tax on buy-to-let property, jewellery and paintings, all unproductive ways to make money compared with investing in productive industry and hard work. Those measures are prudential and, for all the billions of extra revenue they could generate, not explicitly to do with social justice.

The 'tax take' makes little or no difference to overall economic performance. Try as they might, free-market economists have not been able to establish any kind of law linking either high tax take or progressivity in the tax system to low growth in GDP, let alone general prosperity. For all the hullabaloo the UK is not a highly taxed country. Only four of the OECD's thirty member states have a top rate of income tax lower than the UK's. The UK sits in the middle of the OECD's order of countries on the basis of tax take as a proportion of GDP – a position with almost no significance in terms of the UK's comparative economic performance. Most countries have a top rate higher than the UK's in better balanced tax regimes that ensure their wealthy residents pay a fairer share. They may not like it and, as the Liechtenstein story showed, they actively try to conceal their money from the Bundeszentralamt für Steuern and its equivalents. But successful economies have had higher top-income rates, and there is no linear connection between tax rates and growth in GDP.

What needs to be done

A higher top tax band would help rebalance the tax take.
Other countries make their wealthiest citizens contribute more
than the UK's and it does them no demonstrable harm in the
growth stakes. The UK tax system has fallen, by accident and
design, from progressivity into proportionality. Adam Lent,
TUC chief economist, estimates that earnings above £55,000
are taxed at a flat rate. That is as far as progressivity goes. Is
the UK economy so peculiarly constituted – for example, in the
preponderance of financial institutions – that to make it func-
tion, it needs to be less fair? There is no evidence that having a
largish financial sector implies you need to have a less progressive tax regime. A 50% top rate would bring in extra
revenue but, as important, would reshape the distribution of
post-tax income. Imposed on earnings over £100,000 a year,
this increment would produce £4.5 billion a year, on a 2007
calculus. Compare that with the £14 billion awarded in boardroom bonuses that year. Some 1.5% of the working-age
population, about 550,000 people, earn over £100,000 a
year – though many of those earn only relatively small sums
above the £100,000 threshold that would attract more tax.

With this tax band the system would be a little more progressive: the balance of taxes, which shifted away from the
wealthy onto the rest under Mrs Thatcher, would be redressed.
Thatcher didn't cut taxes overall; they rose by 3% of GDP
during her time. She reduced tax on income and increased it on
consumption, which hit the least well off, and Labour kept that
trend going. In three successive manifestos the party pledged
not to raise income tax rates: indeed, on Labour's watch the
basic rate dropped from 23% to 20%, though National

Insurance rose by 1%. The net effect over the years is that lower earners pay a higher proportion of their incomes in tax than higher earners, as VAT levied at a flat 17% takes a higher toll on their incomes than on those of the rich. In the Commons Labour backbenchers once laughed and cheered, pointing at the Opposition, gleeful at Gordon Brown's sheer cheek when he stole the Tories' clothes and cut the basic rate of income tax in the 2000 budget. Yet in doing so they condoned increasing regressivity in the tax system, making it more unfair, which has had to be mitigated by deploying tax credits. It is exceedingly difficult ever to raise tax rates: making cuts without a quid pro quo at the top of the income tax scale was reckless. Labour has lost its fiscal identity, the most fundamental expression of whose interests it represents, whose side it is on.

Increasing the top rate of income tax would raise enough to move towards Labour's child-poverty target and provide more for education or social programmes for poor children. The menu of choices is wide: raising higher-rate tax could permit tax reductions at lower levels. Spending increases on social programmes do not necessitate an increase in the tax take; they could be paid for by realigning domestic spending – though of course every programme, such as health, has its vociferous advocates.

Earmarking taxes on the rich to give poor children a better start in life would make it clear what the money is for. This would be a Robin Hood transfer, taxing the rich for a purpose. Evidence from polling and focus groups suggests 'hypothecation', pegging money to a particular purpose, is most favoured by those who otherwise resist tax increases. It has however been traditionally resisted by the Treasury, which dislikes permanent commitments of spending. The road fund tax is a case in point: originally the annual licence fee payable on each vehicle was money for roads, but over the years the fund was pilfered by the Treasury for other pressing purposes. National Insurance is a fiscal myth; citizens do not pay into or take out of a fund. Yet as chancellor, Brown sold the idea that NI payments would be earmarked for the NHS. Here de facto was an increase in income tax, yet it proved not just politically saleable but popular as well. His 2000 budget adding 1p to NI was the most popular for twenty-five years as a tax-for-good-purposes budget. Labour failed to learn from the lesson. A marginal increase in tax on the successful to pay for better opportunities for other people's children could be generally popular.

Inheritance tax cuts need to be reversed, or the wealth divide across the generations will worsen. Taxation of inheritance, often dated to the succession duty first levied in 1853, was a device for redistributing feudal wealth and great estates long before socialism was a political possibility. Pro-market liberals confess sheepishly that taxing the passage of assets from one generation to the next is a brilliant way of lessening the effect of good fortune and spreading opportunity. Historically it has always been a tax just for the rich, with only one in sixteen estates paying any death duties. Most people pass on their property before they die, downsizing their homes, giving money to children and grandchildren, or they spend it to supplement pensions or care costs.

In the eight years after 1997, house prices rose across the UK by an average 10% a year. Housing now makes up half of total household wealth. Inheritance tax (IHT) used to be payable at 40% on estates worth more than £300,000 and because the threshold for IHT was not lifted as fast as house prices, more people feared their own estates would pay tax: at one stage there was wild tabloid talk of 4 million home-owners becoming liable. But only if they all died at once today. In the real world, people go on living and they spend or give away most of it before they die. What's more, as in the past, incoming chancellors would go on indexing the threshold: no chancellor would survive politically if this tax for the rich began to hit genuine Middle Englanders. But once the scare was raised, tax on estates at death came to be seen as an infernal device to rob ordinary families on their parents' death.

Our man inside HMRC says that avoiding inheritance tax is 'part of the national psyche of the reasonably wealthy'. They play a cat-and-mouse game because avoiding tax is expected by their offspring and seen as a parental duty. Uncorrected by ministers who dared not utter fiscal truths, people even believe that it is a double tax, as it taxes money that has already paid tax. This last is absurd: VAT and petrol tax are also paid out of already taxed income – and most of the value of a home on death has never been taxed at all. But, typically, the Labour government allowed itself to be panicked and, in the face of a concerted campaign by the right-wing papers, fell to emulating the Tories. When in 2007 the Tories promised to raise the IHT threshold to £1 million (£2 million for tax-planning couples), Brown put up the tax-free rate to £700,000 for couples. It was a blind concession to the wealthy. Only 6% of estates, 38,000 in number, were due to pay IHT in 2006–7, raising around £4 billion. HMRC reckoned, in its estimate of the tax gap, it was probably losing the same amount through avoidance. Even if IHT were levied on twice as many estates – say one in eight – it would remain a puny tax on wealth. But the case for extending IHT depends on reforming the way we pay for decent standards of social care in old age; perhaps earmarking a portion of the proceeds of IHT for much-needed care for the elderly is the way forward.

Spreading property ownership to all and applying a property tax is a part of the same policy on inter-generational wealth. Property has created one of the deepest and most bitter divisions in the UK. House-price inflation has impeded social mobility, as the children of those without homes to remortgage can't afford to get on the ladder. It has probably reduced productivity by discouraging those who would have to move to take new opportunities. Key-worker and shared-equity schemes are only marginally helpful: there are too few of them to make much difference. The property boom deepened inequality, encouraged reckless borrowing and distorted the allocation of resources between the different forms of saving; it is now contaminating the debate about tax and equality.

City bonuses have inflated London prices, an effect which has ricocheted to other cities. One bonus boy bought a whole terrace of houses in Doncaster. Houses have become piggy banks instead of roofs for those who need them. House prices are the national obsession of those lucky enough to own their home, a lust that now has more television programmes devoted to it than sex.

Tax is a way to restore the equilibrium to the savings and pensions markets, and to unblock bottlenecks in the supply of housing and urban infrastructure. Many countries – including most US states – tax property as wealth. In Washington DC all those in homes priced above the average pay a tax of 0.8% of capital value every year – which is usually a great deal less than the annual increase in value. The UK tax code was itself once more rational and taxed the benefits that owner-occupiers get relative to those who pay rent.

Nowadays, the small tax that remains on property is highly regressive. Council tax largely lets the wealthy off as the top band is capped at well below the value of expensive houses. It should be removed, so they pay a fairer rate. Stamp duty is anomalous, leaving inheritance tax as almost the only way that domestic property has contributed to the common funds. The case has to be made now. Untaxed gains from home-ownership fuel house-price inflation, encourage property speculation and, above all, widen the gap between the families with and without property. During the boom decade, earning an average of £50 a day untaxed for sitting in a property and doing nothing was just not fair. Politicians need to make that argument.

Fairness is not just about taxes but about securing a living wage at a decent rate families can survive on. Over time pay for carers and clerks needs to draw closer to pay for lawyers and consultants. The minimum wage is the mechanism for establishing a baseline for civilized employment. But enforcement is minimal. Barely 125 compliance officers cover the whole UK. HMRC has only ever prosecuted two cheating employers – a nursery employing childcarers at below the minimum, and Torbay Council. Our request to accompany officials on a visit to a suspect company was refused on the grounds that under existing rules they would be required to warn the employers in advance. How unlike the police, who can invite the cameras to watch them smash down doors and make arrests without jeopardizing the innocent-till-proved guilty status of those snatched from their beds. The system has odd exemptions. Restaurants have a legal loop-hole: recently a restaurant chain was discovered to be paying its waiting staff only £3.75 an hour, well below the minimum wage. But take-home pay was topped up to the legal threshold by tips – and that is legal, so watch out whom you tip.

Other EU countries have vigorous work inspectorates to enforce minimum pay and work conditions laws, but Labour ministers chose a soft regime, afraid of being accused by the CBI of adding regulatory burdens. With £5,000 as the maximum penalty until 2008, when that cap was finally removed, rogue employers have not felt threatened. Legislation now covers the operation of gangmasters, but only in agriculture. Illegal employment helps keep pay low in caring, cleaning, catering and hospitality: big-brand companies use agencies as cover for their bad employment practices, as indeed often do local and central government employers. The Low Pay Commission interviewed staff working for cheating employers. Most knew little or nothing about their rights; they were made to work extra, unpaid hours with large deductions for uniforms and live-in accommodation. Those who rebelled and reported their firms to the revenue were persecuted, and few ever received arrears due even after inspectors found in their favour. The research suggests vastly more abuse than is admitted. A tougher work inspectorate is needed for another reason: illegal work in the UK is the greatest magnet for undocumented immigrants, whose numbers excite alarm. People come here because it's so easy to find no-questions-asked jobs, and that puts a downward pressure on pay rates as well as upward pressure on migration numbers.

The minimum wage is not yet a decent wage, one that will secure a basic standard of living for a family with children. In London a 'living wage' has been set by the campaigning group London Citizens, calculating what it costs to support a couple and two children at a basic decency rate, currently £7.20 an hour. London Citizens, an umbrella of faith groups, churches, mosques and trade unions founded first in the East End, persuaded the mayor of London to set this living wage as the minimum for directly employed Greater London Authority staff and for the staff of contractors. Now London Citizens has persuaded Barclays bank, HSBC, Westfield – the developers of the vast new West London shopping mall – and the Hilton Hotels Group to pay the living wage. This campaign is modelled on one in the United States where sixty towns and cities have signed up to pay the living wage for staff and contractors, including Baltimore, Chicago, Detroit and Denver.

The UK is earning a reputation as an offshore banana republic, the EU's Third World, service-sector sweat shop. Trade unions have argued hard for a law to give the 1.4 million agency workers the right to the same pay and holidays as those doing the same job as permanent employees, but the government has strongly resisted and vetoed EU legislation. Both Blair and Brown always praised a flexible (under-inspected and under-unionized) labour market, which they sought to impress on the rest of the EU. In spring 2008, Brown sought to placate rebellious Labour backbenchers by offering a review. Some right-wing economists claim a large black economy turbo-powers growth, undercutting pay in the legitimate economy, keeping wages and inflation low. But they rarely ask the counter-factual question of how much growth, prosperity and aggregate well-being would ensue if the low paid were less badly off and their lives and their children's lives improved. The CBI doesn't speak for all or even most large companies: reputable companies, such as Hilton Hotels, which has signed up to pay the living wage, rightly see bad employers that undercut on pay as unfair competition that should be driven out of business.

Women's unequal pay means they form the majority of those earning the minimum. Over thirty years ago the Equal Pay Act was passed by Barbara Castle, and those who fought for it thought that the law would fix things, but progress has been painfully slow. In 2007 women working full-time still earn 17% less than men per hour and part-timers earn 36% less an hour. Many women are breadwinners bringing up children alone with no maintenance from fathers; unless they can earn a breadwinner's pay, their children will stay poor. On retirement, women have 40% less pension than men. Women have failed to make enough fuss about equal pay and it needs a full-scale government assault. Every employer should be legally obliged to carry out a pay audit to check the relative earnings of women and men. Secrecy means many women have no idea how they stand in relation to the men doing similar jobs.

In a grim circularity of cause and effect, five sectors – cleaning, catering, caring, clerical and check-out jobs – are less well paid because these are traditional women's jobs. The few men who take such work are demoted to women's rank; only when men outnumber women in any occupation have pay rates tended to rise. The care assistant doing everything all day for frail old people is paid less per hour than the repair man or the gardener outside the window. It can be fixed – but the price will have to be paid. Equality costs, as local authorities are discovering after a raft of equal-pay cases has exposed a backlog of debts they owe their women staff for having illegally underpaid them over the years.

Higher up the social scale, graduate jobs are rarely part-time, so women with children returning to work are obliged to take lower-paid jobs far below their skills and experience. Half of graduate mothers move down to jobs where the average employee at their level does not have A-levels.[4] Along with an assumption that all parents and carers can ask to work flexible hours, there needs to be an assumption that all jobs advertised can be done part-time by two people, except where employers can show reasons why it would be impossible.

Tax credits need to rise. Tax credits have been the great dam holding back growing inequality, channelling money to lower-income families and pensioners. Despite much-publicized administrative difficulties, credits have raised children out of poverty and buoyed the incomes of poor working households, a successful and sizeable redistribution well-targeted at those who need money the most. It is through tax credits mainly that the pledge to abolish child poverty by 2020 is likely to be redeemed, and they would cost £28 billion more a year. It needs £3.4 million to hit the halfway mark by 2010. Out of total government spending of around £500 billion a year, it is under a third of the annual cost of the NHS, six times the cost of running the prisons and three quarters of the defence budget. It would buy the proud boast of living in a land where no child is poor. Remember too, if low pay is raised over the years, tax credits should shrink back to form a less important part of family incomes.

None of this is revolutionary, though to suggest any tax rise has become a political anathema. These proposals would shift income and wealth distribution only modestly. They are relatively small and symbolic changes, most of them taking steps to do no more than restore a balance that has been eroded over the last thirty years. Even if all these were implemented, the UK would still be among the less equal of the OECD nations.

But these measures are significant because they are counter-intuitive, turning the tide on current conventional wisdom. Those FTSE chief executives would still be hugely richer than the average, let alone the low-paid citizen. The gap between them and ordinary people would still be vastly greater than it was thirty years ago. But at least fairer distribution would be on the public radar and more people might discuss how other

European countries have combined greater equality with comparable economic performance and better public services.

Making the case for these reforms would change the political terms of engagement and bring out into the open some hard fiscal truths. Studies suggest that 'poverty' is no longer the right word to use – words such as decency, inclusion, life chances and basic standards resonate better with public feelings.[5] Whatever the language, the case for its abolition remains the same. Research shows that the public respond to functional and moral arguments – reducing crime and anti-social behaviour and increasing fairness. Talk up the good that tax credits do, and how well families spend it. Talk up Sure Start and good parenting programmes. Talk up the idea that children really can be rescued from certain failure, and people are enthusiastic. New awareness might cure the paralysis of nerve, the motor neurone deficiency that has transfixed the politicians, mesmerized by the last decade's cascades of cash. To those who think it impossible, ask this: if none of this, then what would you do to slow the coming social rupture?

The politicians must dare to say boo to the golden geese and regain their democratic authority. Within a generation or two a country could throw off dysfunctional inequality and enervating social discontent and become a fairer, less angry place. Other countries have already been down this path. Most of the rest of Europe and especially the Nordic nations have been consistently more successful economically than the UK, yet have chosen to share the proceeds of success more fairly. Here, the case has been allowed to go by default. There really could be no poor children, none destined to fail from their first breath because of the family they were born into. The Emilys and Callums could enter life's starting gate closer together.

Epilogue

Writing this book, we were told time and again: 'We agree with your analysis but nothing can be done.' Circumstances, however, are changing fast, and what looked close to impossible in 2007 seems much more plausible in the middle of 2008. The cooling economic climate has forced fresh thinking about pay, taxation and fairness, and across Europe executive rewards have come under scrutiny. In May, Joaquin Almunia, the monetary affairs commissioner of the European Union, insisted that moderation and productivity on the office and shop floor had to be matched in the boardroom. Within days, the president of Germany – a Christian Democrat and former head of the International Monetary Fund – railed at 'the grotesquely high compensation of individual finance managers' (*Financial Times*). At a meeting of European finance ministers the same month, the chairman, Jean-Claude Juncker, called for tax increases to curb what he called the 'social scourge' of the excess pay awarded to corporate bosses. UK politicians have been less outspoken, yet here too the credit crunch has provoked a re-examination of the financial sector. Even commentators on the centre right, from Martin Wolf in the *Financial Times* to Alex Brummer in the *Daily Mail*, welcomed this turning of the tide. If the jobs, incomes, homes and prospects of ordinary people are going to be hurt, how much is being paid out in boardrooms and bonuses becomes a legitimate public concern. Words not often heard in recent years – 'fairness' and 'social justice' – started appearing in reports.

Labour's blunder over the 10 pence starting rate for income tax crystallized the new public concern. Inadvertently, on the back of this political catastrophe, Labour succeeded in pro-pelling its traditional concerns over poverty and inequality into mainstream national consciousness. During the spring and summer of 2008, in the backwash of the subprime mortgage crisis in the US, an increase in the tax paid by the poorest stirred a wave of popular anger about fairness. Announced in Gordon Brown's last budget as chancellor, the ploy of cutting tax rates for everyone at the expense of imposing more tax on the poor-est became apparent only when low-paid employees opened their pay packets in April. It was as if a dam had burst. House prices (stagnating and threatening to fall), the environment (oil prices spiked), and the gap between the economic fate of those at the top compared with those at the bottom were loudly debated. At a by-election, Labour lost a safe seat in Crewe and Nantwich, where that injustice to the lowest paid became the first reason people gave for switching away from Labour in an 18% swing of anger and revulsion. It levered the lid off other questions, and what had been taboo could now be openly talked about. How were public demands for more and better social care in old age to be paid for? It was legitimate for right, left and centre at least to consider inheritance tax and whether it should be pegged to care. Voters' anger at the Labour government concealed a rediscovery of the relationship between the tax system and social justice. The threat of recession has rekindled a sentiment of solidarity. If hardship must be borne as the cost of necessities rise, then it should be shared more fairly, and not fall most heavily on the weakest shoulders. With the governor of the Bank of England bemoaning greed among bankers and the leader of the Conservative Party regretting child poverty and shrinking social mobility, it's clear that new possibilities for policy have opened up.

The excuses and self-justifications of the boom years have started to implode. The high priests of globalization and mega-rewards, the consultants McKinsey, revealed in May the findings of a survey of managers at multinationals, commenting that 'The movement of employees between countries is still surprisingly limited' ('Why multinationals struggle to manage talent', *McKinsey Quarterly*). In which case, how had they got away with all that cant about the need to inflate salaries and bonuses to attract the globe's finest managers and to prevent executives fleeing overseas?

In April Mervyn King, the governor of the Bank of England, so quiet while company boards were paying themselves fortunes for footling corporate achievements, found his voice when he gave evidence to the Commons Treasury committee. Bonuses in banking, he intoned, were excessive. Even the head of the CBI, Richard Lambert, has admitted (*Guardian*, 23 April) that

Epilogue

the bonus culture in the City and on Wall Street was responsible for the excessive risk-taking that led to the collapse of the US mortgage market.

Even as he spoke, new figures for the first part of the 2007–8 bonus season emerged. Between December 2007 and April 2008, facing global and banking turmoil, the City still looked after itself very well indeed. Our *Guardian* colleague Ashley Seager calculated that some 1,040,000 people in the finance sector shared in a bonus pool worth £9.8bn in the three months to February 2008. What's striking is not that the total is down on the comparable three months in 2006–7, but that it was down by only 5%. If the credit crunch has been hurting since at least August 2007, the banks and finance houses have been oddly slow in cutting back. No one pretended the battle for sanity and proportion in boardroom remuneration was going to be easy, or quickly won. The total packages of the chief executives of the thirty biggest UK companies rose by a staggering 33% during 2007–8, according to a study by consultants (*Financial Times*, 23 May).

The political and public mood is shifting. A *Financial Times*/Harris poll taken across countries in Europe, Asia and the US in May found public opinion 'strikingly consistent': large majorities were saying the gap between the rich and the poor was too wide, including 74% in Britain. Even in America, 'traditionally seen as more tolerant of income inequality', 78% now said the gap was too wide. The poll also found that 'clear majorities' across all the countries surveyed believe that 'taxes should be raised on the rich and lowered on the poor'. In the chill of financial crisis and economic slowdown, fairness matters more than it has for a long while. In straitened times, poorer people will need more, not less, protection; the best off should contribute most. This is no longer a simple left-versus-right political cause, as all parties feel the need to respond to the public mood. The instinct for fairness is hard-wired into people, and so into all democratic politics – more than ever in times of adversity.

Acknowledgements

We would like to thank all our interviewees, some of whom opened their doors knowing the resulting reports were unlikely to be favourable.

Acknowledgement is due to the partners and senior executives in the firms where we conducted our conversations with high earners for securing our access to their colleagues – they must remain anonymous. That research, carried out by Ipsos Mori, was generously supported by the Joseph Rowntree Foundation and the Barrow Cadbury Trust and we would like to thank their respective directors, Julia Unwin and Sukhvinder Stubbs, for responding with interest and enthusiasm to our project. They bear no responsibility for any of our conclusions.

Notes

Introduction

1 Institute of Fiscal Studies, *Racing away?: Income equality and the evolution of high incomes*, Briefing Notes BN76, January 2008.

2 John Plender, *Going off the Rails: Global capital and the crisis of legitimacy*, John Wiley, 2003.

3 John Hills, *Inequality and the State*, Oxford University Press, 2004.

4 Dominic Hobson, *The National Wealth: Who gets what in Britain*, HarperCollins, 1999.

5 Gary Solon, *Nature and Nurture in the Intergenerational Transmission of Socioeconomic Status: Evidence from Swedish children and their biological and rearing parents*, National Bureau of Economic Research working paper 12985, 2007.

6 *The Class Divide*, BBC Analysis, 9/11/06 (bbc.co.uk/nol/shared/spl/hi/programmes/analysis/transcripts/09_11_06.txt).

7 *Child Poverty in Perspective: An overview of child well-being in rich countries*, Innocenti Report Card, UNICEF, 2007.

Notes

8 Avner Offer, *The Challenge of Affluence*, Oxford University Press, 2006.

Chapter 1

1 *Understanding Attitudes to Poverty in the UK*, Joseph Rowntree Foundation, 2007; *Public Attitudes to Economic Inequality*, Joseph Rowntree Foundation, 2007.

2 *Inequality and Quiescence: A continuing conundrum*, Institute for Social and Economic Research, University of Essex, 2007.

Chapter 2

1 J. K. Galbraith, *The New Industrial State*, Princeton University Press, 1967.

2 Michael Blastland and Andrew Dilnot, *The Tiger that Isn't: Seeing through a world of numbers*, Profile Books, 2007.

3 Rakesh Khurana, *Searching for a Corporate Saviour: The irrational quest for charismatic CEOs*, Princeton University Press, 2002.

Chapter 3

1 British Social Attitudes, *The 22nd Report*, Sage Publications, 2005.

2 *Narrowing the Gap: The commission on life chances and child poverty*, Fabian Society, 2006.

3 *A More Equal Society?: New Labour, poverty and exclusion*, Policy Press, 2005.

Chapter 4

1 *Breakthrough Britain: Ending the cost of social breakdown*, Social Justice Policy Group (chair: Iain Duncan Smith), 2007.

Notes

2 *Families at Risk*, Cabinet Office Social Exclusion Task Force, 2007.

3 *Ends and Means: Future roles of social housing in England*, Centre for the Analysis of Social Exclusion, London School of Economics, 2007.

4 Stein Ringen, *What Democracy is For*, Princeton University Press, 2007.

5 *Indices of Deprivation*, Office of the Deputy Prime Minister, 2000.

6 *Purse to Wallet?: Gender inequalities and income distribution within families on benefit*, Policy Studies Institute, 1998; *Welfare Reforms and Child Wellbeing in the US and UK*, Centre for the Analysis of Social Exclusion, Paper 126, London School of Economics, 2007.

7 *Families and the State: Two-way support and responsibilities*, Commission on Families and the Well-Being of Children, Policy Press, 2007.

8 *Marital Splits and Income Chances over the Longer Term*, Institute for Social and Economic Research, University of Essex, 2008.

Chapter 5

1 *Life Chances and Social Mobility: An overview of the evidence*, Prime Minister's Strategy Unit, 2004.

2 *Inequality in the Early Cognitive Development of British Children in the 1970 Cohort, Economica*, vol. 70, pp. 73–97, 2003.

3 Betty Hart and Todd Risley, *Meaningful Differences in the Everyday Experience of Young American Children*, Brookes Publishing, 1995.

Notes

4 Gosta Esping-Andersen, 'Social Inheritance and Equal Opportunity Policies', in *Maintaining Momentum: Promoting social mobility and life chances from early years to adulthood*, Institute for Public Policy Research, 2005.

Chapter 6

1 Jo Blanden et al, *Intergenerational Mobility in Europe and North America*, Centre for Economic Performance, London School of Economics, 2005.

2 John Goldthorpe, 'Intergenerational Class Mobility in Contemporary Britain: Political concerns and empirical findings', *British Journal of Sociology*, vol. 58, issue 4, pp 525–46, 2007.

3 Jo Blanden and Steve Gibbons, *The Persistence of Poverty Across Generations*, Policy Press, 2006.

4 John Goldthorpe et al, *Education-based Meritocracy: The barriers to its realisation*, Nuffield College paper, 2002.

5 *Intergenerational Transmission of Disadvantage: Mobility or immobility across generations? A review of the evidence for OECD countries*, OECD, 2007.

6 *Intergenerational Mobility and Assortative Mating in Britain*, Institute for Social and Economic Research, University of Essex, 2002.

Chapter 7

1 Sir Peter Gershon, *Releasing Resources for the Front Line*, HM Treasury, 2004.

2 *The Impact of Sure Start Local Programmes on Three-year-olds and Their Families*, National Evaluation of Sure Start, HMSO, 2008.

Notes

Chapter 8

1 *Attention-deficit Hyperactivity Disorder*, National Institute for Health and Clinical Excellence, 2005 (nice.org.uk/guidance/index.jsp?action-byID&r=true&0=11632).

2 *Public Service Productivity: Education*, Office for National Statistics, 2005.

3 *Evaluation of Reading Recovery in London Schools: Every child a reader 2005–2006*, London University Institute of Education, 2006.

Chapter 9

1 *Low Wage America*, Russell Sage Foundation, 2003.

Chapter 10

1 *Fit for Work: Musculoskeletal disorders and labour market participation*, Work Foundation, 2007.

Chapter 11

1 Laura Edwards, *A Bit Rich?: What the wealthy think about giving*, Institute for Public Policy Research, 2002.

2 *Should Egalitarians Expropriate Philanthropists?*, Centre for Economic Policy Research, 2007 (cepr.org/pubs/dps/DP6362.asp.asp).

Chapter 13

1 Lord Sainsbury, *Race to the Top: A review of government's science and innovation policies*, HM Treasury, 2007.

2 Nick Ellison, *The Transformation of Welfare States*, Routledge, 2005.

Notes

3 Richard Murphy, *The Missing Billions: The UK tax gap*, TUC, 2008 (tuc.org.uk/economy/tuc-14238-f0.cfm).

4 'Moving Down?: Women's part-time work and occupational change in Britain 1991–2001', *The Economic Journal*, vol. 118, no. 526, 2008.

5 *Understanding Attitudes to Poverty in the UK*, Joseph Rowntree Foundation, 2007.

Index

242

Index

Index

Index

Index

Index

Index